Sculpting Space in the Theater

Design: Red Design

Focal Press is an imprint of Elsevier
30 Corporate Drive, Suite 400,
Burlington, MA 01803, USA
Linacre House, Jordan Hill,
Oxford OX2 8DP, UK

RotoVision SA
Sales and Editorial Office
Sheridan House, 114 Western Road
Hove BN3 1DD, UK
Tel: +44 (0)1273 72 72 68
Fax: +44 (0) 1273 72 72 69

Library of Congress Cataloging-in-Publication Data

British Library Cataloguing-in-Publication Data
A catalogue record for this book is available from the British Library.

ISBN 13: 978-0-240-80866-6
ISBN 10: 0-240-80866-5

For information on all Focal Press publications visit our website at www.books.elsevier.com

05 06 07 08 09 10
10 9 8 7 6 5 4 3 2 1

Reprographics in Singapore
by ProVision Pte

Printing in China by Midas Printing International Ltd.

Sculpting Space in the Theater

Conversations with the top set, light and costume designers

Babak Ebrahimian

Contents

Introduction

There can be nothing more exciting than the act of interpreting and creating a world. You take an empty space and shine a light on it: suddenly a form or shape is born. You look out the window and there are thousands of people in different costumes, walking up and down and across the street. You sit down in a café or restaurant or you look up at the sky at the universe and stars, and you find a world carved out and specifically designed. Regardless of the nature of that world's creation—natural or made by human hand—and the time of its creation, your eyes meet space, time, and a world of design wherever they look.

The stage of the theater or opera is not that different. Imagination works as a facility of the human mind to carve, shape, and sculpt spaces, shapes, and forms. This creation process and its final realization are what is commonly referred to as design. The world of design in the theater and opera is vast and endless. For every piece, each designer will have a different approach, philosophy, style, and process. As a given rule of aesthetics, no two designers are alike, and their designs will forever hold their own unique signature.

The goal of this book is to emphasize and highlight the primary importance of design and designers in the world of theater and opera. Anyone with a love for these arts cannot but have a natural curiosity about their design. It is design that—along with the actors—fills the space and tells the story. Shakespeare or Beckett, Mozart or Wagner, small or large, simple or complex: the space of the stage will need a design, and designers tell the story as much as actors do. Without design, directors, producers, and actors would not be able to give full shape or life to the story. In short, design is instrumental to the creation, interpretation, and staging of any piece. *Hamlet* needs a place and a space to stand on. He needs clothes to wear, and ultimately he needs to be seen.

How then are these questions addressed? Set, costume, and light design are the bold answers, but exactly how are they thought about, designed, and implemented for the stage?

Going back to the mid-20th century, notable directors and designers have often formed a close-knit unit: Bertolt Brecht and Caspar Neher, Giorgio Strehler and Luciano Damiani, Heiner Müller and Erich Wonder are but a few. In some cases, directors are also designers: this is true of Robert Wilson. In other cases, designers are not only theater and opera designers, but also design for movies: this is true of Santo Loquasto, who is a collaborator on and designer for Woody Allen's movies. No matter how one looks at it, all great and memorable productions of the theater and opera stage have been the result of successful collaborations with designers.

Finally, beyond the stage, many designers are teachers and mentors of design at some of the top design schools: they help shape the next generation of designers. This is true of Ming Cho Lee, who is co-chair of the design department at Yale School of Drama, and Susan Hilferty, who is the chair of the design program at Tisch School of the Arts at New York University—to name just two.

How then does design work? What is the starting point? How do designers think? How do they actualize their visions and thoughts into a three-dimensional space? And how is design taught and thought about in advanced design classes and programs?

Looking at the visual world of stage design, the top designers in the fields of set, lighting, and costume design were asked about their philosophy, their approach, and their thoughts on design. The following interviews were all based on the same structure and questions, giving each designer full rein to answer as they wished.

Each interview began with the same questions: "What is your starting point for your design?" and "What are the elements that make for a good design?" The designers were then asked to elaborate on questions such as "How would you design *Hamlet*?" or "*Waiting for Godot*?" Designers who also teach and mentor students in design were asked to explain their approach and their philosophy of design. Looking at the interviews, the reader will notice how the different designers have informed and influenced one another across the generations.

Each of the designers described their understanding, process, and approach to design, and supplemented this with anecdotes and examples to make their design world more tangible for the reader. In some cases the designers reflect on the relationship between the set, the lights, and the costumes, and how the different elements interact with one another. Some muse on the radical changes they have undergone since their early days, while others illuminate the differences between working with European and American directors and theaters. Each designer brings his or her own voice and area of expertise to this book, making them vivid and approachable.

It has been an immense honor to meet these designers in person and catch a glimpse of how they work and think. In most cases the interviews quickly became a substantial exchange and encounter, where the designers freely and generously discussed the art, craft, and philosophy behind their design. I am forever grateful to all the designers interviewed in this book—John Lee Beatty, Howell Binkley, John Conklin, Beverly Emmons, Susan Hilferty, Constance Hoffman, Ming Cho Lee, Adrianne Lobel, Santo Loquasto, Jennifer Tipton, George Tsypin, and Robert Wilson—for their time and willingness to discuss their understanding of design and its process. Without their generous contribution, this book would not have been possible.

Thanks also go to the Byrd Hoffman Foundation, the Metropolitan Opera, the San Francisco Opera, and the Shakespeare Theatre Company for supplying images for the book; to Ottessa Moshfegh and Simona Schneider for their work on transcriptions; and to Alex Young for supporting the project. I also would like to thank my editor at RotoVision, Lindy Dunlop, for her assistance and guidance throughout the process; her help and advice have been invaluable.

This book is for Esther.

Set Design
John Lee
Beatty

Sketches often hold the essence of John Lee Beatty's designs. Here he discusses the emotional impact of his sets, and explains how—through a series of drawings and quick sketches—his designs materialize. The model for a production too, he explains, arises from the two-dimensional drawing.

A Delicate Balance, Edward Albee. *Plymouth Theater, New York, USA, 1997. Directed by Gerald Gutierrez. Design based on Dorothy Rogers'* A House in my Head. *Design not approved by Albee.*

Introduction

Two essential facts come out of this interview with John Lee Beatty. The first is that he is interested in creating an emotional response with his sets among his audiences; the second is that he works best through sketches and two-dimensional representations of the plays he designs. Models are built, but only after the two-dimensional sketches—for Beatty, models are too much like toys and do not give an accurate reflection of the dimensions.

Beatty, whose sketches often reflect a three-dimensional space, also talks about the importance of a ground plan and how that plan is a significant step for him in creating the set.

Burn This, Lanford Wilson.

Designed for The Mark Taper Forum, Los Angeles, and for the Plymouth Theater, New York, USA, 1987. Directed by Marshall W. Mason. Color rendering of a choreographer's loft in lower Manhattan. This thrust design was later transformed for proscenium on Broadway.

The Caretaker, Harold Pinter.

Roundabout's American Airlines Theatre, New York, USA, 2003. Directed by David Jones. In this first pencil sketch, an angled room gains a roof gable and furniture, and actor placement is experimented with.

Approach

In the case of *Hamlet*, which is a familiar classic—slightly different from getting a new play—I read the play. I read it once only for content, and then I go back and read it again for what the designer needs to do. I break it into scenes, review what each scene has in it and what I think the problems are, and any questionable activities. When you read a play, as a designer, your approach is somewhat different from that of the author. It's a huge collaboration: you are collaborating with the author and trying to present them properly.

Even with *Hamlet* you have to say, "What is the best way to make this author's goal achievable, and is there anything we can do to accentuate the positives and ease our way through the more difficult phases?" How you are going to present the ghost is clearly one of the important decisions. How do you help the actor playing the ghost not to get laughed at? How do you enable today's audience to accept the ghost? Is there any way the set can help that presentation of the ghost to be achieved by allowing the play to go forward without people saying, "Hold it a second, this isn't working for me"?

At a certain point, whether that's the designer's or director's job becomes a big blur. A successful relationship with a director and a script and a lighting designer is a collaboration.

The set designer's role

I would say the job description of a set designer is: what does it look like? How big is it? How does it sit in a theater? Very basic questions, and sometimes after answering those three questions, your work is basically done. *Hamlet* is an interesting one because clearly there is a real Elsinore. I was in Elsinore once when I was eight years old, so I have preconceptions of what it looks like. Also, Shakespeare did not visit Elsinore, that we know of, so what did he think it looked like? Was he using it as a metaphor for another court that might look much more English? Who knows? There is all that to explore. And if, for preliminary research, I were to fly to Elsinore to look at it, it might be very misleading and not really go to the heart of the play at all. Perhaps it would be extraneous information that is confusing.

And the time that I am living in right now also comes into play. I was looking at some stills of the movie of *Hamlet* recently, and thinking how interesting it was that their early Fifties romanticism permeates their take on Elsinore. They thought it should have a forbidding, slightly exotic Scandinavian history to it, while the Elsinore we know is plainer and more neo-classical. Their interpretation reflected their own time as much as the time of the play.

"Exploring where you are going to go is always the interesting part."

012

The Rivals, Richard Bringley Sheridan.
Vivian Beaumont Theater, Lincoln Center, New York, USA, 2004. Directed by Mark Lamos. A thrust design for the city of Bath. A doughnut revolve brings furniture out of the various doors.

And in terms of size, how big is *Hamlet*? You could do an enormous amount of work. I could be designing an entire palace of Elsinore, and the director and I could look at it and say, "Look where that table is sitting, right there—isn't that good?" And then we could decide that we don't need the rest of it. That is entirely possible.

I mean, I will do an entire color sketch of something and we will decide not to do it, and people will say, "Oh, it's horrible, all that work lost." But it isn't work lost, because you went there in terms of the sketch and saw what the production might look like, and then you decided that's not it, but you took away from it the sense of being there. In some shows I even ended up just making do with black masking; or you might go in the other direction just to go back to the black masking. And you have learned something in the process; it is not a useless activity, because exploring where you are going to go is always the interesting part.

Sketching the design

After I've read the play and charted it out in scenes and acts, I personally draw sceneries instead of constructing models, so I start drawing sketches. Almost like sub-sketches: a little idea, a little plan, just casually. Sometimes I sing or say things to myself while I draw. Sooner or later I show a few of these ideas to the director and we talk. It is like an actor reading a play in front of the director for the first time. You are very embarrassed, because you want the sketch to be wonderful, but of course you are trying to find out what it is first. The director has to listen to you, and I talk about things that bother me or that I don't think I'm finding—very much like an actor. Then the little drawings start getting more evolved. It is a gradual progression until something comes out fairly fully.

The drawings are in black and white, and gradually emerge in color toward the end. One problem you have when drawing for a director is that if they feel you have gone to the trouble of drawing something, and you draw it too well or use all the colored paint the first time, they might think, "Oh, I am offending him" and speak too carefully. So if I have done a color drawing, I will purposely destroy it in front of them so that they know it's okay to let loose. And the drawings are mainly for me: I want to see what it would look like if I did this, this, and this. Sometimes things are thrown out totally. I often keep the original black and white sketches because later on, when you are going into the final stages of designing, they are very useful. Or if the show gets into trouble, you want to go back and see what it is that you were trying to do, so that there is more clarity to the work as to what you intended when you started out. Sometimes it is a lot clearer in the original pencil or pen drawing than it is in a full-color model or sketch.

Going back and forth with the director over the designs and sketches takes as long as it takes. Sometimes it goes very quickly, but it could go on for a couple of months or for a couple of days.

I do somewhere between two and 20 drawings in the process. In one particular show that had 17 we were very far along and the author disagreed with something. The director and producer and I agreed, but the author didn't, so we went back and did it again, and everything seemed to be going okay. Then the director approved something and I said, "Guess what? We have a new problem. I don't like it." So then I had to go back myself and find something that I liked, that the director liked, that we all agreed on.

Choice of play

I like a mix of plays and a mix of theaters. I think the biggest variable for me as a designer—and I am an American designer working in American theater, which is an important point if you look at my work—is whether it's a play that's been done before or whether it's new. Certainly, with a play that has been done before, you become aware of other productions, or there is a general idea about how it should be done. But with a new play that is not the case, and you are floating out there by yourself. Personally, I find that situation fascinating. What I have

"Good design is when the fit of the design and the material is such that one can't tell where one stops and the other begins."

The Caretaker, Harold Pinter. *Roundabout's American Airlines Theatre, New York, USA, 2003. Directed by David Jones. A revised rough sketch with prop notes, and a new axis and door placement.*

The Caretaker, Harold Pinter. *Roundabout's American Airlines Theatre, New York, USA, 2003. Directed by David Jones. Approved rough sketch includes concealed exits and entrances so the actors will not be silhouetted crossing in front of the now central window.*

found is that people are far more willing to experiment on a classic, or on a play that has been done successfully before, than they are to experiment on a new play, because with a new play everyone is so nervous they would prefer to do something conservative just to get the play on. It's not a time for experimentation. A lot of people think that doing a new play itself is, in itself, enough of an experiment.

On what makes a good design

For me, a good design is when the fit of the design and the material is such that one can't tell where one stops and the other begins, and where the physical and visual worlds are a perfect mesh. I don't mean mesh as in a picture of the perfect environment, but where the evolution of the movement of the actors within the scenery—and the light changing within the scenery, and the costumes—is on a parallel track with the play, without being redundant to it. So that the way that you feel about the space, and the look of the space, has the same emotional richness the play itself has, without merely duplicating the author's work. People say that you don't really notice the details in the scenery, or that only the set designer recognizes them. I don't think this is true. I have done some productions where all I did was fix up the architecture of the building and left the stage alone. I am very much aware that theater has a wonderful and horrible quality that it is totally evanescent, in that it is going to go away. I am a fairly classical designer, but I am aware that we live in the moment, and what you think about a set five years from now is really irrelevant. I am not designing for posterity.

I think I am an interpretive artist, so everything affects me. I designed *Dinner at Eight*, which took place on Park Avenue, and two or three times I walked up Park Avenue at night after another show; and I more or less realized that I wasn't researching the buildings, but was pondering what it meant to live on Park Avenue and how I felt walking down the streets. And I think it showed up in the design because there was a kind of odd darkness—a nighttime quality to the design—that came from that experience. And an appreciation of the play's interesting blend of comedy and sadness came from those walks.

On associative thinking

One of the fun things about being a designer is that you don't know where the designs come from—they just come out. I always say I am an associative thinker. I remember sitting with Harold Pinter once, and we were talking about a play that he was directing, and I told him the drapes were brown. It was a goofy thing to say, but I knew that the drapes were brown, so I was sharing that information with him. And he looked at me rather oddly. How did I know the drapes were brown? I don't know, but I knew the drapes were brown. It is an interesting thing; you just have to let yourself go there.

For example, in the play *Proof*, which was a new play that I designed first off Broadway and then on, one day I said to the director, "Would you mind if I put autumn leaves all over the set?" He said that was fine, and I realized I brought to the play a sort of autumnal color scheme and an autumnal sense. But the play takes place in many different years and different times of the year. I clearly felt that the play was a bit of a romance in the sense that it was a fiction, and in the sense that it was a romantic story about love. It had an autumnal quality, and that is what I brought to it emotionally; that clearly showed up. I don't think the author states it in the play, and the director never said that it was an autumnal romance; that is just what came out of me.

Sometimes there are technical things that you have to do as well. There are quick changes that you don't want to feel are quick changes. I was designing a technically sophisticated ground plan that looked simple from the front, but was actually more complicated when you dealt with the actors' needs, in terms of making the show seem effortless. And when you

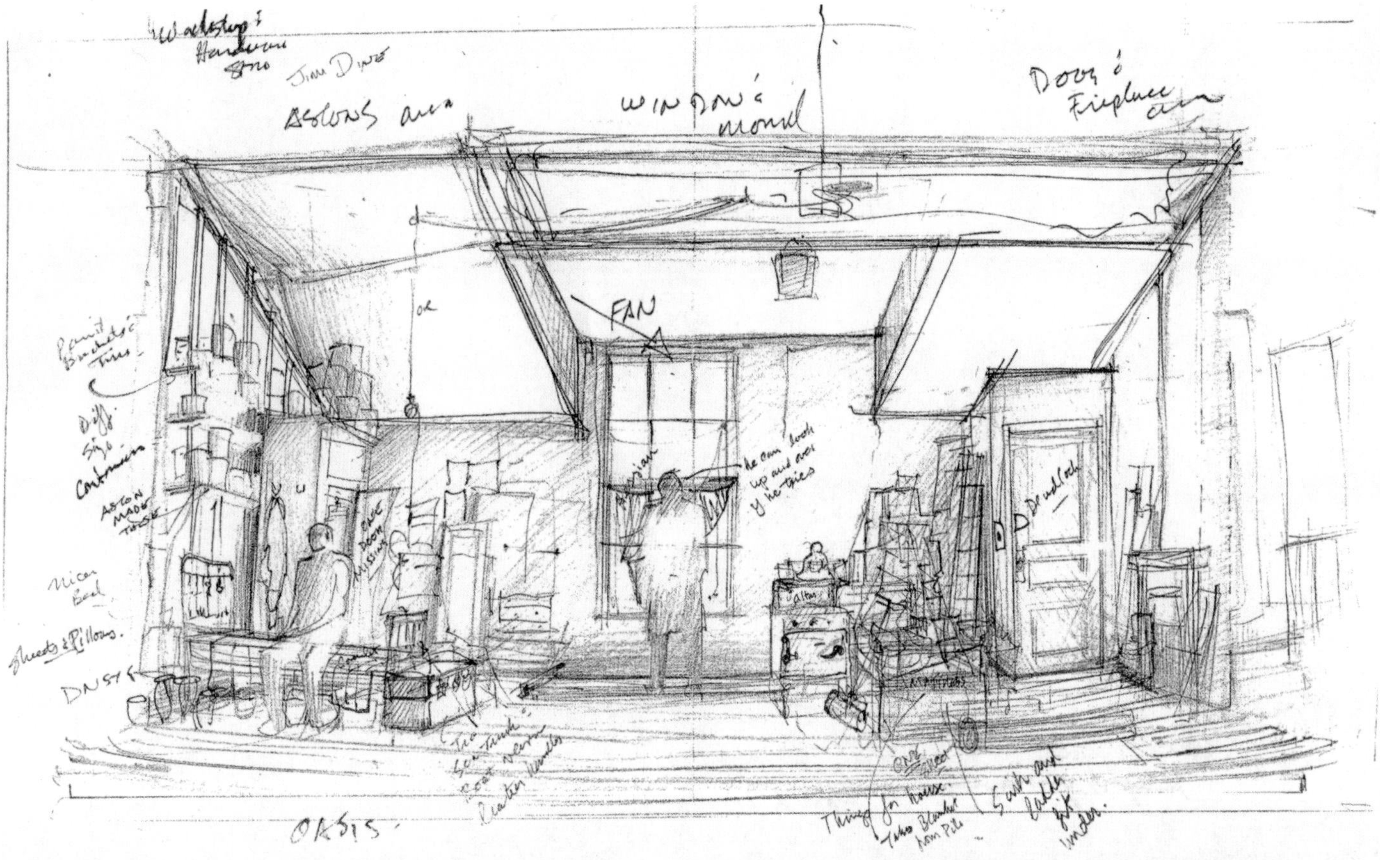

Workshop & Hardware Store

Jim Dine

ASTONS area

WINDOW & mood

DOOR & Fireplace area

FAN

Sheets & Pillows.

OASIS.

"THE CARETAKER" BY H. PINTER

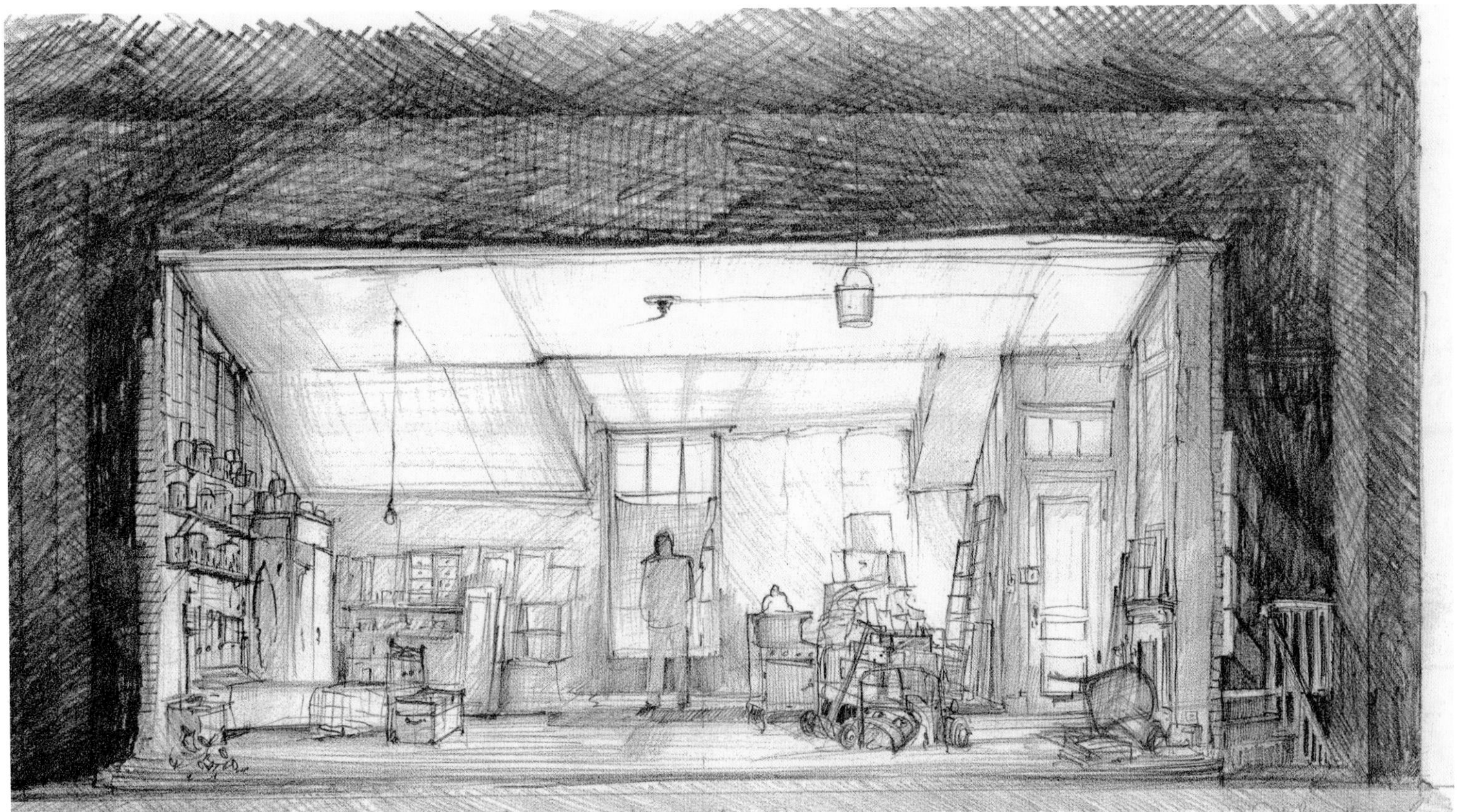

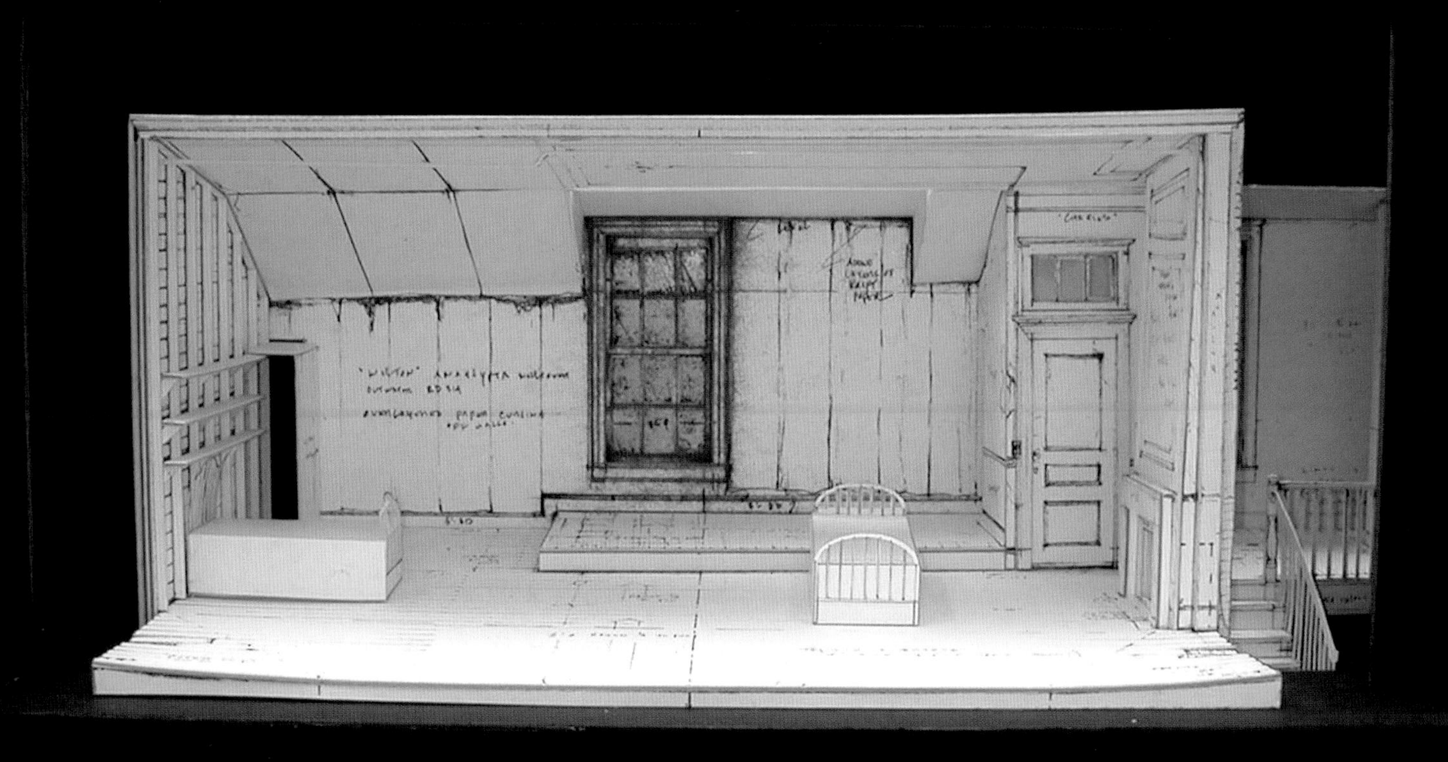

"From my earliest experiences I have been fascinated by how an inanimate object can create an emotional response."

have those emotions, you are instinctively creating spaces that have possibilities for certain kinds of movement. Or you are instinctively adding things to the environment that the actors might use or not use. It might even become part of the text of the show.

Good design is when you end up instinctively providing the proper space for the play. One play I think I did well on was *Burn This* by Lanford Wilson, where I instinctively added a fire escape and access to the fire escape. It ended up that the actors and director and author found ways of using the fire escape that weren't in the script, but by the time the play came to life you would never do it without the fire escape—or the space that the fire escape was, in both senses: the literal space and the alternative space it provided for the actor. There was a need for an alternative space that you just didn't know about.

On emotional impact

Designing is an emotional experience. It is only three percent of my work, the designing part, and the rest is execution. Those moments of knowing where you are going to go are the interesting emotional moments. There are times when I don't feel like it, and times when you can't. I come from an ethnic group that doesn't prize emotion as virtue, so I think some people would be surprised to hear I have emotions at all. I feel as if I am communicating emotions through physical representations or environments, or the shape of the set we are looking at.

That is my basic feeling about what I do. An actor conveys emotion on stage. An author certainly conveys emotion, and a director creates emotion. I create emotion too. From my earliest experiences I have been fascinated by how an inanimate object can create an emotional response in the viewer. I create an emotional temperature for plays, and when I get it right it's very good, and when it isn't, it is wrong.

I have trouble doing plays to which I don't have any emotional response. Gerald Gutierrez and I did a production of *The Most Happy Fellow* on Broadway and it was very interesting. Musical theater has emotions built into it. There's a place in the music, and he and I found out that if you moved a part of the scenery during a certain part of the music, the audience would cry. We learned to experiment with the moment that piece of scenery moved and whether the audience would cry. It turned out there were two places in the music when you could move it and they would cry—but some would only cry when the scenery moved as well as the music. Literally, a piece of plywood moving at a certain moment will create an emotional response.

People critique my work and they always say, "He does those rooms where you want to move in," or "It reminds you of your childhood." Certainly, those are emotions that I want to be there with the actor. Sometimes just a shape can create a certain emotional environment for the actor. It creates a tone for the way the performance has to be given, created, presented.

The designer's signature

Some designers can be recognized by their designs. I once saw a musical in London, and I walked in off the street at the last moment and didn't get to read the program. The lights went down and they started singing, and I was looking at the lights and thinking that whoever designed this had a lot of nerve. It looked just like … And I pulled out the program and, sure enough, it was Pat Collins. It was so funny to me that I recognized her in her lighting. And that also happened to me with a costume-designer friend. I saw a brief snip of a movie—I didn't know what the movie was. There was an actor leaving a car and going into a house. I called my friend, the designer, and said, "Was some movie that you designed on TV last night?" She confirmed that it was. Some designers' personalities show up, as Ming's does. You can clearly see Ming Cho Lee-ness in things. You don't really know what their personality is like, but you know what their artistic personality is. Having Ming as a teacher is like going into the

The Caretaker, Harold Pinter. *Roundabout's American Airlines Theatre, New York, USA, 2003. Directed by David Jones. Color rendering showing lighting and paint effects based on the style of Lucian Freud and Edouard Vuillard.*

The Caretaker, Harold Pinter. *Roundabout's American Airlines Theatre, New York, USA, 2003. Directed by David Jones. White model created from the designer's drafting to be used by the director, stage manager, and builders. This version shown minus the prop-dressing pieces.*

"Sometimes, being realistic about the theater, doing a not very interesting design job with an interesting group of people is more rewarding than creating a delicious set with less exciting collaborators."

A Delicate Balance, Edward Albee. *Plymouth Theater, New York, USA, 1997. Directed by Gerald Gutierrez. Approved final color design rendering of the living room of a wealthy house in Westchester. The set has nine visible areas, each painted and lit successively cooler as they retreat from the audience.*

A Delicate Balance, Edward Albee. *Plymouth Theater, New York, USA, 1997. Directed by Gerald Gutierrez. The set on the stage of the Plymouth Theater built with a raked deck and extreme forced perspective.*

studio of a Renaissance master and, while you are painting for Leonardo, you paint like Leonardo. And when you leave, it is fascinating to see what is left in you and what drops away, and what else you find in yourself as you go along. You wouldn't be doing him any favors if you ended up just like him; that wasn't the point in the first place.

I think people make assumptions about me from seeing my work. I am typecast for doing realistic interiors—or what people call realistic interiors—but I don't agree with that. I would say representational interiors that have a certain emotional warmth or coldness: something you can respond to. Now, I am going by things other people have told me, but a sense of completeness to the world that I create.

On designing Beckett

If I was asked to do *Waiting for Godot,* I wouldn't know how I would design it until I know what the production is and who's working on it. I don't have any predictions. I think I would be tempted to read the play again. That particular play, like *Hamlet,* is something that is fairly familiar to all of us. So it gives you some leeway. There would be the question of what to do about the tree. I would think about it for a long time. Start asking questions. I think the more interesting question would be: if *Waiting for Godot* came along as a new play and had never been produced before, what would I do? I don't know. That playwright is notoriously particular about what you do with his work, but I don't think it would terrify me. I mean, it is always terrifying to design. It is an enormous responsibility not to screw up.

We already know that *Waiting for Godot* works. Like *Hamlet,* we know it is a valuable play, so not necessarily as difficult as designing for something that might turn out to be not so valuable. There is nothing worse than working on a play and then realizing halfway through that the play isn't up to it at all and is not going to succeed. At which point, the designer or director might try to gloss over the fact as part of their duty toward the producer. You try to make a successful evening, even if it is not a successful work. Which is hard to do. The truth will out, usually.

As for the tree, the author has told you it is a tree. You don't have to wonder whether there is a tree; he has been quite specific. I think it would be a lot harder if the playwright hadn't made it clear whether there is a tree or not. And that play may be successful because there is a certain clarity to the author's work. The more interesting question would be: does the tree exist? Let's slide into *Hamlet* again and ask if the ghost exists? I guess the author says it does in some form. The more interesting question is: if you thought the tree or the ghost was inappropriate, what would you do as a designer? This is sometimes the case with a new play.

Personal preferences

A play I would really love to design is *The Way of the World* by William Congreve. And I would like to design the musical *Showboat.* There are certain plays I am interested in too. Sometimes being in the room with a certain group of people working on a play can be as interesting as the design of the play. There are certain plays where the design isn't an especially fascinating activity, but the play itself might be interesting to work on, so you have to measure one against the other. Sometimes, being realistic about the theater, doing a not very interesting design job with an interesting group of people is more rewarding than creating a delicious set with less exciting collaborators.

Opera has never come after me. And I don't do many musicals. Another successful American designer in my shoes would have done more musicals than I have. The ones I have done, and that have been successful, have been incredibly minimal. I find that interesting, because knowing me as a designer, it is interesting to reconcile the designs of *Ain't Misbehavin'* and

"I have a classicist's sense of plan, and there is a clean plan to all my work."

Chicago with the other work that I do. They are equally a part of me, but seemingly contradictory in approach. I would say what both have in common is a certain clarity of design that permeates all my work. I have a classicist's sense of plan, and there is a clean plan to all my work. I just can't stand bad plans.

The purity of the ground plan of *Chicago* and the ground plan of *Talley's Folly* is equally clear. I don't think anyone would consider the two in any way similar, but they are in their clarity of plan. You as an audience member, through the clarity of the plan, know where you are. I always want the audience to relax: not relax as in go to sleep, but more in the sense of knowing where they stand in the universe so that they can concentrate on what is being presented in front of them.

You can have plenty of detail and let people discover it later, but the basic information needs to be committed easily. In fact, I sometimes try to draw the set quickly—in less than a minute, or less than 15 seconds really. If I can't draw what it really is, that is a problem.

On models and artificiality

I do make models. Oddly enough, I imagine in sketch form. I know that scenery is sculptural, but I do it all backward. I mean, I imagine in three dimensions clearly—in texture and sculpture—but I imagine all of that better in two dimensions. I go into it emotionally, but to me a model is a bit of a toy, because it is miniature. It is misleading because you can't tell how big things are. I am very concerned with scale and with the size of the actor and the size of the theater. Models don't help me; they help other people.

I almost surprised myself the other day. Somebody said, "We need to do this to get people to come to the theater," and I said, "If they don't want to come, don't force it. If they don't want theater, that's fine. There doesn't have to be theater." But it doesn't seem to be a problem so far. Theater just morphs into something else that people do want. The theater district is usually near the red-light district. It is a socially acceptable vice, really. I don't think it hurts you. I get off on the artificiality of it.

It is all an artificial construct. Even when you see a realistic play, it is still artificial. It is a fun thing in that way. I mean, art is artificial too. Art: you make a piece out of something. Oil paint is made out of chemicals. Theater is made out of different things too.

On changing theater styles

I am fascinated by the way theater changes; backstage and on stage. Our tastes and our goals as human beings change. Overall I think our theater, like politics, veers left and right, but goes in a gradual arc. One of the more interesting things in my lifetime has been this "Oh, we hate the proscenium," "Now we love the proscenium," "Now we have to build everything in thrust." We have to do classical theater or angry theater … And then all of a sudden you are doing plays with people sitting on sofas, talking to each other again, and the worst kind of theater to build for is a thrust theater [one in which a raised platform extends into the auditorium, allowing the audience to surround the stage on three sides.] I find that really interesting: how we have gone away from the proscenium and come back to it in my lifetime. It is fascinating the way styles and tastes come and go.

I don't like spaces that give the wrong information. I don't like working in theaters where it looks like there is a lot of backstage space when there isn't. Or vice versa. I like it when the stage and auditorium space are either one or seem to be appropriately matched to each other. The most successful theaters I have been in have little to do with comfort, and more to do with a good fit between stage and audience. That's the best kind of theater; the format of the theater does not matter to me.

Biography

John Lee Beatty has designed some 70 shows for Broadway, and has been equally busy off-Broadway and in the regional theaters. He first gained recognition for his work at Circle Repertory, where he designed the premieres of many plays by Lanford Wilson. Later work has included premieres of plays by Arthur Miller, Tennessee Williams, Beth Henley, Terrence McNally, Wendy Wasserstein, Neil Simon, David Mamet, John Robin Baitz, and John Patrick Shanley, as well as numerous New York premieres of international works. On Broadway he has designed *The Color Purple, Rabbit Hole, The Odd Couple, Doubt, Who's Afraid of Virginia Woolf?, The Retreat from Moscow, Wonderful Town, Frankie and Johnny, Proof, Chicago, Twentieth Century, Major Barbara, The Last Night of Ballyhoo, Anna Christie, Redwood Curtain,* and many others. For Lincoln Center Theater he has designed *The Rivals, Big Bill, Dinner at Eight, Morning's at Seven, Spinning into Butter, Ring Round the Moon, Ivanov, The Little Foxes, An American Daughter, A Delicate Balance, The Heiress, Abe Lincoln in Illinois, The Sisters Rosensweig,* among others. Among his off-Broadway productions have been *Defiance, Engaged, House and Garden, My Old Lady, Book of Days, Sylvia, Mystery of Irma Vep, Comic Potential, Lips Together, Teeth Apart, The Destiny of Me, The Road to Mecca, Song of Singapore, Ashes, A Life in the Theater, Aristocrats,* and *The Miss Firecracker Contest.* He has devised all of the City Center *Encores!* concerts. A winner of the Tony, Obie, Drama Desk, Outer Critics Circle, and Joseph Jefferson Awards and a member of the Theater Hall of Fame, Beatty is a graduate of Brown University and the Yale School of Drama.

Howell Binkley

Lighting Design

What makes Howell Binkley an outstanding lighting designer is his ability to design for Robert Wilson as well as for productions on Broadway and off-Broadway. Here he discusses lighting design and how, regardless of whether the production is a dance piece or a Broadway show, the two have certain basic elements in common. If lighting a dance piece is sculpting space in the abstract, then lighting a Broadway show is sculpting space in a tangible manner. Both approaches, however, have the same basic principles.

Jersey Boys, Bob Gaudio and Bob Crewe.

August Wilson Theatre, New York, USA, 2005. Directed by Des McAnuff.

Introduction

Talking about lighting design, Howell Binkley starts off by discussing the knowledge acquired from designing the empty spaces of dance concerts. For him, lighting is "creating the scenery and the whole footprint for the choreography." He then describes his work with dance concerts and dance companies, before talking about lighting a space like Broadway, which has scenery and is not an empty space.

When you get to a space with a lot of scenery, you have to "dissect" the "real estate" of the space in order to know where a light can be hung. Based on this real estate of the stage, designing the lights for a production is then made possible. But, as Binkley points out, what makes for a good design is ultimately the designer's instincts and art as a designer.

Jersey Boys, Bob Gaudio and Bob Crewe.
August Wilson Theatre, New York, USA, 2005. Directed by Des McAnuff.

Jersey Boys, Bob Gaudio and Bob Crewe.
August Wilson Theatre, New York, USA, 2005. Directed by Des McAnuff.

"The lighting is creating the scenery and the whole footprint for the choreography."

Approach

Dance is pretty much my roots, but in the beginning, working alone on a dance piece, you're really dealing with a raw space. A lot of the dance that I've done in my career has been with no scenery at all. So what the lighting is doing is creating the scenery and the whole footprint for the choreography. I think one of the most challenging things about being a lighting designer is being able to sculpt a space with no scenery at all, and being able to give it an environment that relates from the choreography to the music to what the audience is seeing.

I did a piece that David Parsons choreographed; I'm a co-founding member of his company—he and I started the company in 1986. He has a piece called *Caught* and it's done with strobe lights, and he is always caught in the air; you never see the dancer hit the ground. So we're sculpting a space with strobe lights that always show the dancer suspended in the air, whether he's upside down or straight up, whether he's walking or horizontal. We made this piece in 1982 with gracious grants from friends of ours, who gave us enough money at that point in our careers to make this piece happen.

There are other pieces that I do where there's no scenery and I've got to establish a framework for the audience to see what the choreographer is doing. And I think there are a lot of incredible dance lighting designers, and we all put that challenge upon ourselves: to create an environment for the choreography to be seen by the audience. It is really a collaboration between yourself and the choreographer about where you want this piece located: is it outside, inside, in a very isolated area? It's all about what the audience is going to see. I think that's the place to start, because they're paying money for the ticket, and you want to give them an environment and let the choreography make that journey—that arc—through what the choreographer is trying to do with his work.

Dissecting the space

To me, it's about more than sculpting. Before you get to the sculpting element of it, you have to dissect your space—your real estate on the stage. Where can you hang lights? Where do they hit the dancer, or the actor, or the scenery? I think scenery and technology and automation have, over the last 20 years, gone overboard, in a good way. We now have automated lighting, we have computers, we have scenery that moves with computers … So first of all, as a lighting designer doing a big show with a lot of scenery, you have to establish your real estate on that stage: where you will be able to enhance the scenery and sculpt into the space.

Dracula, Frank Wildhorn, Don Black, and Christopher Hampton. *Belasco Theatre, New York, USA, 2004. Directed by Des McAnuff.*

Dracula, Frank Wildhorn, Don Black, and Christopher Hampton. *Belasco Theatre, New York, USA, 2004. Directed by Des McAnuff.*

"I love doing all the dance projects when there is no scenery and there is a lot of room for light and air, to light the air, to light the space ... to follow the dancer in a certain way."

Maybe I'm using the wrong word—it's really figuring out your real estate to dissect the way you can break up your stage. As lighting designers, we work for months and months on a model, and do final drawings and things get approved, and then we lay it down on a table and start drafting it. And that's where the magic comes from, while you establish that real estate where you can hang your tools. Your lights are your tools in the sculpting process, and you're designing, but it's really dissecting your space and how you want to treat and move each scene along. A lot of the shows and musicals we do will have 34 scenes in the first act, whereas some shows will have 34 scenes in total. You have to be able to move the show on, to arc it from A to B, so that it's seamless.

When I say real estate, I basically mean the stage, but when it's full of scenery and drops, you have to be able to squeeze lights in between that, and sometimes we're not given that. Sometimes—and it's not a bad thing—it's a battle just to get 30 inches here or half a pipe, or a boom in there or a sidelight position. Today there's usually a deck of about eight inches, so that we can put a lot of lights in the floor cued up, which doesn't affect the scenery at all, except for being out of the way of automation tracks that go across the stage, or up and down the stage. Today there's a lot of scenery on stage.

I just did this production of *Dracula* at the Balasco—and there's a lot of beautiful scenery that comes up through the deck, plus there are three fully flying rigs that each take up 30 inches. So three times 30 inches: I could have electrics in that, but I can't, because there are humans flying in there, and they've got to mount, fly, and release from their harness. So today real estate is a key issue for us in doing our work. Sometimes we say, "Could you just scoot this upstage three inches!" And sometimes three inches might turn into two and a half—it does get to be a battle, but it is a collaborative battle.

On no-scenery and scenery sets

I love doing all the dance projects when there is no scenery and there is a lot of room for light and air, to light the air, to light the space … to follow the dancer in a certain way.

I think both the no-scenery approach and the scenery approach are alive and can coexist. In a lot of shows you will see a great deal of scenery and all this spectacular flying stuff. Then all of a sudden the scenery evaporates, and there's just lighting: a quiet moment when all the scenery is gone—there's a duet, there's a solo … And that is the magic of what we do. We can create a moment of tenderness out of nothing, just with the light and the actors.

"Broadway is the crème de la crème of what we do, but we've all paid our dues through diverse projects that challenge us and make us the different types of designers that we are."

The shows are so big now that we have to form a seamless arc: we have to do transitions, lighting-wise, where scenery is moving upstage and there's a book scene downstage—we have to keep that book scene alive, and hide what's happening upstage. We have to highlight, take the audience's eye and focus it on a point, while behind them things are changing that we have to mask.

On lighting challenges

In *Dracula*, in the beginning, the director said, "I don't want to see any lines on any of the people flying." And you did not see one line at all. These people were suspended in the air and flying, and you never saw a line to their bodies. And that is the kind of challenge that we're up against—that's a creative challenge between the lighting designer, costume designer, and set designer. That's a design challenge. It's where you put your lighting. It's about your levels, your intensity, your color, your angle—especially with a body that moves. If it's stationary, it's a piece of cake. But when it's going up and down, up and down, and flipping—that's difficult. But that's why we're hired to do our craft, and that's why we're trusted by directors and choreographers to achieve their vision. But they're also letting us bring our visionary tools in, to dissect a show.

It's amazing today, the scale at which we all work: being able to keep those nice tender isolated scenes, with just a chandelier and little chairs, and then suddenly it all opens up and you're in a seaport. It's the layering—after you dissect a show you have to layer it, and that's where that sculpting element comes in. You've got to give light to every scene, and you have to make it work where there is not a scene, which I call a transition.

Broadway and beyond

I do tons of regional work around the country, tons of off-off-Broadway work … but I take a Broadway element into it. Whether we're in Washington, Walla Walla, or Chicago doesn't matter to me. We're craftsmen, designers, and we're hired to be there, probably because of a director we've worked with for years. Whether we're in a 10 x 10 space that has no fly gallery or whatever, you have to be ready to attack anything. And that's what makes us who we are. Going into a garage theater and doing a musical when you only have 20 lights, you've got to stretch your imagination. And less is more. It's not like on Broadway, where you can have a lot of tools. Even here in New York there are very small spaces, but people are still coming to see the work and your name is involved with it.

I don't think Broadway spoils us. I hope not. Maybe I'm speaking for myself, but I think I'm speaking for a lot of other people too. Broadway is the crème de la crème of what we do, but we've all paid our dues through diverse projects that challenge us and make us the different types of designers that we are. Look at Jennifer Tipton, Kim Billington, Jules Fisher and Peggy Eisenhauer, Don Holder, Brian MacDevitt, Natasha Katz, Ken Poser … They've all had a journey, and they've all been different and taken a different path. But if you put them all together, you'd see that there's a lot of similarity between each person's path and how they've gotten where they are today.

The secret of good design

When I feel good about my work is when I feel that it's been a collaborative process. When you're cueing strokes, you're cueing integrity, your looks have all worked with the scenery, the clothes, the sound, and the transitions have all been (and I use this word a lot) seamless, or noticeable—however the director has conceived it or the book has been written …

So I feel good about my work when it's a collaborative unity. I'm not in it for me; I'm in it for the product, for the show, for the work. We all spend very long hours in the theater, in a dark theater, even before the actors arrive. We spend hours and weeks and months, sometimes, on pre-preparation. A set could be designed and approved, but then it's over budget. So there have got to be cuts, and we've got to redo. There's revision after revision, re-meeting after re-meeting. There are conference calls, emails—there are a lot of components that happen before the show even loads into the theater. You get in, you do your craft and when it's collaborative, it's smooth—and that's when I feel most gracious about what I do. And that happens almost 100 percent of the time, I feel that good about what I do and the people I work with. An outstanding design comes from your instinct, and your art as a designer.

Biography

Howell Binkley's many Broadway shows include *Bridge and Tunnel, Jersey Boys, Steel Magnolias, Dracula, Ave Q, Golda's Balcony, The Look of Love, Hollywood Arms, The Full Monty,* Gore Vidal's *The Best Man, Minnelli on Minnelli, Parade, Kiss of the Spider Woman, My Thing of Love, Sacrilege, Taking Sides, High Society, How to Succeed … , Grease,* and *Sinatra at Radio City.* Off-Broadway he has done lighting for *Radiant Baby, Batboy: The Musical, the New York Shakespeare Festival, Playwrights' Horizons,* and *City Center Encores!* He has also designed around the country at La Jolla, the Shakespeare Theatre, DC, the Old Globe, the Guthrie, the Goodman, Hartford Stage, and the Sondheim Celebration at the Kennedy Center. In addition Binkley has designed lighting for dance and opera companies such as the American Ballet Theatre, Parsons Dance Company (co-founder), Joffrey Ballet, Alvin Ailey, Houston Ballet, Metropolitan Opera, and Dallas Opera. He was the recipient of the 1993 Sir Laurence Olivier Award.

John Conklin

Set and Costume Design

An avid reader of texts and theories about texts, John Conklin discusses his approach to theater design—for both set and costumes—based on understanding the text and questioning it from as many angles as possible in order to fully understand, appreciate, and decode the meaning of the play or opera. Within Conklin's approach, if listening to a piece of music can help in understanding the text of a play, that too can be factored in as part of the design process.

The Ring Cycle,
Richard Wagner.
San Francisco Opera, USA, 1985. Directed by Nicholas Lehnoff. Set and costume design, John Conklin. The last scene of Das Reingold *(Act IV): The gods entering Valhalla.*

Introduction

For John Conklin, the world of the text is open to interpretation. Rather than abusing this openness, he feels it must be carefully dissected in order to reach the full meaning of the play or opera before designing it.

Conklin, who is a professor at the Tisch School of the Arts, carefully goes through his process of questioning *Hamlet* and *Waiting for Godot* to illustrate the way he approaches the text prior to designing it. Is there really a tree in *Waiting for Godot*, or is it merely a stage direction? How do stage directions come into play in the reading of a text, and how does one design them? Looking at various philosophical approaches to the text and text analysis, Conklin shows the mastery of a designer who is capable of designing any text, from *Hamlet* to *Waiting for Godot* and Robert Wilson's *The Magic Flute.*

The Ring Cycle, Richard Wagner. *San Francisco Opera, USA, 1985. Directed by Nicholas Lehnoff. Set and costume design, John Conklin. A model study:* Die Walküre *(Act III).*

The Ring Cycle, Richard Wagner. *San Francisco Opera, USA, 1985. Directed by Nicholas Lehnoff. Set and costume design, John Conklin. A model study:* Reingold *(Act IV). Valhalla is based on the 19th-century architects Schinkel and von Klenze.*

"My sets and set design can be characterized as more architectural than painterly."

Approach

My sets and set design can be characterized as more architectural than painterly. By that I mean using actual dimensional architectural forms to delineate space. These may be distorted or expressionistic, depending on the effect desired.

Working with the director is of course the primary collaboration, but all the other designers (costume, light, and, increasingly, sound) are also crucial. We constantly strive to meet together, because the world we are attempting to create is made up of many different components that all influence each other. And through discussion those elements can shift and change direction—often in radical ways. When this happens, you want it to occur in a group, so that the decisions are mutual and organic. You work in a circle in an attempt to go straight ahead.

Working with the text

The starting place is always the text. All understanding is connected to one's experience, but there are certainly tools by which you can begin to analyze a text, starting with what is often referred to as "close reading." There are clusters of metaphors, recurring imagery, and key words.

Take *Hamlet*, for instance: a play full of disease imagery, metaphors of acting and performance, references to mirrors, reflection, and portraiture. You study the overall structure of the piece. I have my students at NYU (New York University) make what we call a "fever chart" of the play. Is the play like a descending line? A circle? A chaotic squiggle? Big scene, small scene? Interior, exterior? Endless questions … Why Denmark? Can we postulate what Denmark meant to Shakespeare? What does Denmark mean to us?

Sometimes this comes as a surprise to my students. But, the more you do it and the deeper you go, the more interesting it is. I keep saying to them: even when they are working with directors, they will find that a good director will appreciate a designer being a dramaturg.

By the word "text," I am referring not only to the dialogue, but also to the stage directions, although I question how the stage directions affect the play, because they are not spoken. They are written by the playwright, but so much of it is the author's intention, and so much of the deconstruction says that you should pay no attention to the author's conscious intentions. I don't always completely trust the writer's conscious intentions.

"When you do theater, you learn a lot about what opera can and cannot do; and when you do opera, you learn a lot about what theater can and cannot do."

That doesn't mean you could do anything. You do somehow need to be connected to the text. There are no easy answers to this; it's a constant struggle. And an answer that you find for one production is not even going to be true in three years' time. There are no certainties, because this is a theater event, existing in the present. It is not a novel and it is not like reading a play by yourself; it is a theatrical event with actors and audience.

Moving into the set design

To translate all this into design, you have to create a moment when it begins to go someplace. I find that one way to achieve direction is through music. I often ask a director what the play sounds like, or I explore the play with him through music. Sound as image. Schoenberg or Bach? Schoenberg might lead to Kandinsky. Could that be *Hamlet*? Mad, tortured, impressionistic, fragmented? Or is it a classical world of order and symmetry in which chaos erupts?

Then I start sketching, if I know what theater space it is in. I build very quick, rough models, and then just play around a lot. I cut things out and paste them up, and take straws and pieces of wood or bottle caps, or whatever. Sometimes I have a sort of specific idea, sometimes no definite idea. It depends upon how clearly I see it. Sometimes it comes together right away; sometimes it takes a long time. Sometimes you work and work, and then you throw it all out because it's not gelling. You start again. But you have learned from everything you have thrown out. It is not as if you have wasted your time. You're exploring an undiscovered country.

Theater versus opera

I don't mind whether I design for plays or operas, because I don't think there is much difference between them. They are both basically about people in situations—about drama. The means by which they express them might be different, but the means by which you realize them upon the stage are not that different. There's the whole business about opera being "larger than life," and of course it is in a way; but in another way it isn't, because the scale of opera is the scale of human beings.

In the United States the relationship between opera and theater is not as close among designers, directors, and audiences. In Europe the best directors—Patrice Chereau, Peter Stein—do theater and opera all the time, at the same time. When you do theater, you learn a lot about what opera can and cannot do; and when you do opera, you learn a lot about what theater can and cannot do. A lot of it is figuring out how certain things work on stage. So I think it is a big mistake not to do both all the time. The cultures don't overlap in this country in the same way they do in Europe. And I wish that the audiences overlapped more.

To design *Othello* in the opera (as opposed to *Othello* in the theater), you'd need room for all those choristers ... Instead of 25 people, you need room for 70 people. And you would probably be doing the opera in a bigger theater—and that affects the whole business. The play grows out of an Elizabethan English theater culture, and the opera grows out of a 19th-century Italian opera culture. On the other hand, both Shakespeare and Verdi were singularly great dramatists; therefore they are alike in many ways.

On good design

A design can be "perfect" for a particular production, those actors and that audience at that time. But you don't know what makes it perfect; it's just a mysterious combination. And one person's perfect is another person's mediocrity. When I saw Peter Brook's *Midsummer Night's Dream*, I thought that was a perfect production. It didn't make me say, "I never want to see *Midsummer Night's Dream* again." I have done *Midsummer Night's Dream* a couple of times since then, and I have been able to because everything changes.

The Ring Cycle,
Richard Wagner.
Chicago Lyric Opera, USA, 1992. Directed by August Everding. Set and costume design, John Conklin. Die Walküre *(Act III): Wotan summons Loge, the god of fire.*

The Ring Cycle,
Richard Wagner.
Chicago Lyric Opera, USA, 1992. Directed by August Everding. Set and costume design, John Conklin. The magic fire encircles Brünnhilde.

036

The Ring Cycle,
Richard Wagner.
Chicago Lyric Opera, USA, 1992. Directed by August Everding. Set and costume design, John Conklin.
Siegfried *(Act II): the forest bird leads Siegfried to Brünnhilde.*

"I would say that a design doesn't work when I feel that it hasn't gone deep enough."

I would say that a design doesn't work when I feel that it hasn't gone deep enough—meaning either intellectual or instinctual deepness. I would say that a production doesn't work when either the instincts are not strong enough or the work is not thought out enough. Or there isn't enough time. You are up against pieces of enormous complexity and you have to get as deep into them as you can. And that takes a lot of work and a lot of time.

I don't like design shows or exhibits, because the design does not exist separate from the production. You can look at something and say, "This is very striking" or "This is very evocative," but you are not looking at a painting or a piece of sculpture, or even a building; you are looking at a something that supports a group of actors performing in front of an audience. Sometimes the most striking set will destroy the performance. You don't know how "good" a set is except in the context of the performance.

There are no rules about what makes a good design. You can't meet a checklist, because a set has an organic life. What people should not do is walk out of a show and say, "I really didn't like it, but I loved the set." There is something terribly wrong there. The set cannot be good if the production is not good. The trouble is that sets and costumes do have a material existence—a presence—which by itself can be sensuously or intellectually pleasing, in the same way that a painting can. But that is actually a sort of false existence, because the set only exists within the performance.

You should never see pictures of the set. When I collaborated on the American exhibit in the Prague Quadrennial [the Prague Quadrennial is an international design competition and exhibition], I was determined to do an exhibit that was not about models and sketches. So we did an exhibit that was about process. It was successful; we won the gold medal. I had been to the Prague Quadrennial before and thought, "If I have to look at one more beautiful set with no actors …" Here was this giant building devoted to theater and there were no actors. How could this be? This made no sense to me at all.

On detail

In *Waiting for Godot* the stage directions say there's a tree. But what Vladimir says about the tree is that it looks like a willow, and Estragon says that it looks like a bush. I give that problem to my designers, because I think that it is a very interesting problem. Maybe there's no tree.

The discussion of any specific problem (that damn tree), which you have either with yourself or with your director or fellow designers, can teach you a huge amount about the play. There is no quick answer; so there has got to be debate, discussion, and questioning—and Beckett obviously wants you to do that, because he has two characters talk about the tree and they cannot agree what it looks like. They can't decide who Godot is, and they can't decide what day it is.

Everybody finally has to make a choice. But a choice doesn't need to end the ambiguity, or force it to mean one particular thing. Now, if you make the tree to be what Estragon sees and not what Vladimir sees, you are making a decision that has specific ramifications.

If you have no tree, or a tree that is different from what either of them says they see, what are you stating? That they are mad? That they are creating their own world out of nothing? Isn't that what we all do? Isn't that a definition of art ... of theater? A pessimistic view would say that they are delusional, unable to agree on any basis for rational behavior; an optimistic view that they make up something, invest it with a value system, and are thereby able to exist. Is *Waiting for Godot* an optimistic or pessimistic play? Is *Hamlet* optimistic or pessimistic? I would say somehow both at the same time. This represents not fuzzy thinking on Beckett's or Shakespeare's part, but a great artist's acceptance of the difficult (and comic) ambiguities of our existence. We seem always to want answers—but *Godot* says in effect, "You know guys, there aren't any." That doesn't mean you have to give up; that you don't say anything or do anything. You keep going.

I strongly disagree with directors or designers who explain their "concept" to an audience before the event. The ideas—the "concepts"—exist only in the performance, with all its glorious ambiguity. Each audience member might have to wrestle with the ideas in the same way we did, and then come to their own conclusion.

After all, the theater is all fake, all imagination. I would love to do a production of Beckett that took place on an elaborately naturalistic 19th-century set, just to see what would happen. If you did a minimalist play in such a world, you might get the audience creatively unsettled.

On contemporizing work

I think that when Peter Sellars' opera productions work, they are great. But sometimes they don't work. In order to put opera in a contemporary setting you have to know what the other world might be. Like Picasso—you have to know how to draw like Ingres before you can draw like Picasso. Strong texts can take care of themselves in such a setting. By putting them in a "contrary" setting, you set up a fascinating tension.

It's creative and stimulating, particularly if the piece has become—as *Godot* has—accepted, tamed, and part of our culture. It doesn't have the power to disturb so much anymore. When it was first done, people would walk out and throw their programs on the stage, which is actually a fine reaction. You want somehow to recreate that power. You want to destroy its comfortable surroundings and let it reveal anew its power to disturb. Such disturbance is a good disturbance, because it challenges our complacency.

Concluding the design process

Technically, you end up with a complete set of drafts that a shop could build from, and a complete model that can be painted from. Then you put it into the theater. And then you see what you've got... You add actors, costumes, lights, sound. You are now seeing it in time and in space, and with all the elements, and then you go to work again. What you start with is a proposal: a reasonably certain aim or direction. Sometimes you put it on stage and it doesn't work and you think, "This is never really going to work, so we'll make it as good as possible." Sometimes you say, "This is a total mess and nothing is working, and I know exactly what we should do now." Then you edit and redesign.

Once a production opens, you can't really interfere, because there is no money to make adjustments, to rehearse changes in the tech time available, or to see too late a more fruitful direction that you might have pursued.

Biography

John Conklin has designed sets and costumes for the major American opera houses: New York City Opera, Opera Theatre of St. Louis, the Glimmerglass Opera, and the opera companies of Dallas, Houston, Minneapolis, Washington, Los Angeles, Santa Fe, and Boston. He designed the world premiere of John Corigliano's *The Ghosts of Versailles* and Jonathan Miller's production of *Pelléas et Mélisande* at the Metropolitan Opera, and has completed two *Ring* cycles: at San Francisco, directed by Nichols Lehnhoff, and at the Chicago Lyric Opera, directed by August Everding. In Europe he has worked for the English National Opera, the Royal Opera, Stockholm, the Bastille Paris Opera (costumes for Robert Wilson's *The Magic Flute*), and the opera companies of Munich and Amsterdam. He has also designed for Broadway and off-Broadway (including the Public Theater) and extensively for regional theater, including the American Repertory Theatre, Boston; the Goodman, Chicago; the Hartford Stage Company, Long Wharf, New Haven; the Mark Taper Forum, Los Angeles; the Actors Theatre of Louisville; and Center Stage, Baltimore. He has also designed for dance with such companies as the Joffrey Ballet, Boston Ballet, and the Royal Ballet, London. He teaches at the Tisch School of the Arts, NYU, and serves as Associate Artistic Director of the Glimmerglass Opera.

Beverly Emmons

Lighting Design

Lighting design has its own language. A celebrated designer is one who can speak as many of those languages as fluently as possible. Each production has its own needs, and each director has his or her own approach. Beverly Emmons discusses her work with Liviu Ciulei and Robert Wilson, two directors and theater artists with completely different styles and approaches to the theater.

Aladdin, Alan Menken, Howard Ashman, and Tim Rice.

Children's Theatre of Minneapolis, Minneapolis, USA, 2005. Directed by Matthew Howe. A pink backlight revealed in stage haze announces the arrival of the genii.

Introduction

Designing for two different theater artists with two different backgrounds, approaches, and aesthetics to the theater is an impossible task unless you know his or her design skills, craft, and language of design. Beverly Emmons is one who knows her language well and is capable of designing for as diverse a stage as need be. In this interview she discusses her collaboration with Liviu Ciulei and Robert Wilson, showing how the skills and language of lighting design come into play in working with different artists with different sensitivities.

Emmons also discusses the differences in designing for the European theater versus the American one. That said, the starting point for her design—as with all great designers—is the text, and she points out that, regardless of whether the text is familiar or new to her, she returns to read it before moving on.

Approach

I read the play; even if it's familiar, I'll read it again. I take care not to have opinions. Then I go to the first meeting with the director. Usually, at that point, the universe of the play has already been developed in conversation between the director and scenic designer. The space you ask about is determined by their conversation and by the givens of the theater in which we will play. In a project as familiar and frequently done as *Hamlet*, there are many possible universes ... Are we doing real Gothic castles? Are we doing a bare stage? Are we doing some modern-dress fascist version, setting it in 1930s Germany? There are wild divergences. I mean, what color is the living room: is it soft or is it sharp?

You need to begin to understand the vocabulary of the director. You do that by keeping your mouth shut and asking him what he thinks, and hearing the words he uses to describe what he thinks the play is about, and what he wants the lights to do. Inexperienced directors will sometimes say, "I don't know how to talk to a lighting designer," and my answer is, "I don't want you to worry about that. Keep talking. Say anything that comes into your head. It's my job to understand you." With someone like Liviu Ciulei, because he is a European director, there's also the issue of working style. You look at the expectations of who you're working with.

And then there is the theater, the venue. Where are we? Are we in a university auditorium? Are we in a big commercial venture, with big commercial expectations—they're going to plunk down 10 million dollars and want their money back at least? Or are we at La MaMa? Where can I put lights? How flexible or rigid is the venue? That means both the architecture and the personalities. What is there to work with? That means not only the economic wherewithal, but also the implicit style of the location, as well as the production.

European versus American approaches

In Europe, directors often have a more explicit understanding of lighting because they are often called upon to do it, and to tell the electrician at whatever big theater they're in what they want. The lighting happens as a collaboration between those two guys. I'd heard Americans who've worked with Liviu say, "Oh, he just wants to do it himself." I understood what that meant—to me that meant a stylistic difference between what American designers expect to do, and what European directors expect to do. If you're not aware of that, you might be surprised.

The first time Liviu and I worked together was at the Welsh National Opera. With all the usual expectations, British lighting designers model

"Good European directors are a special case, because they know what they want to see and how to ask for it."

themselves on the working style we created here in America, as independent artists who are going to make the lighting choices themselves. I just made Liviu a Magic Sheet: a little drawing with channels, showing where things were focused and their colors, and I sat back and waited. Liviu began to light the scene, asking for channels and turning things on ... And what I found very amusing was that all the people around me at the tech table were waiting for me to blow up! But eventually of course he got stuck, he couldn't find something, and I said, "Liviu, can I help? I'm here to help!" Around us, everyone relaxed.

Afterward I said, "You don't use me very well. If you had said more to me in rehearsal about the ideas you had, I would have had more of it available for you." So he had to be trained to trust and use American designers, at the same time as American designers were learning to trust him. He knows what he wants: do what he says.

Years later I worked on a small production of his at Lincoln Center Institute and asked a colleague of mine to light it. I looked and thought, "Wow! That looks like the lighting I do," and then I realized, "Of course! It's Liviu's lighting, and he got her to do the same thing he got me to do!" Good European directors are a special case, because they know what they want to see and how to ask for it.

It's the way light shades down a wall and catches a couple of characters sitting in a certain way ... It's not strong colors; it tends to be pale colors. It often has fewer cues, less light moving around pointing at what one should be looking at. The rolling repertory system of much of Europe means that they must refocus every day for each of several productions occurring on the same stage on any given week. The extremely special lighting rigs and exquisitely precise focusing of hundreds of luminaries that we have on Broadway or the West End are only possible when a production is going to play in the same theater by itself for a long time.

Lighting as a secondary art form

Each individual artist has his or her signature. I can go to a colleague's work on Broadway and say, "Yeah, they did it again ... That's what they do: beautiful, fabulous stuff."

Light and scenery and costumes, I like to say of them, "We are secondary art forms." We depend on the primary art form, which is what is happening between the play and the director. Or the choreographer. And we support their ideas. If they don't cook up something good together, nothing we do can help. If a play doesn't have an essential rightness—two people talking to each other in a scene, sitting that way at that emotional point—no amount of lighting will make it right. And often, especially the way we do commercial productions in this country, because they cost so much money, directors are called upon to explain what they're going to do, in order to drum up the finance. But that's very dangerous for an artist. What you have to do is go and make it, because often the description becomes hype; it gets built up and imagined in everyone's mind, and when they finally settle down and go into rehearsal four weeks before previews, what's there is often a very different animal—a small jewel perhaps, and not bad; just different, because of what was found in the script, what the actors did, what was discovered as they worked.

It would be ideal for lighting designers if we could see the piece rehearsed and then design for it. But instead, in the US, we have to have a lighting plot all finished and in the shop before the first day of rehearsal, as if we were creating a building. Then, when it fails, it looks as if it was over-produced. Partly because the designers have to have all their work done before that rehearsal period starts.

"I feel my work is to support and reveal the art, in whatever circumstances we find ourselves. For me, it depends on figuring out what the art is in advance of it existing."

You're designing what the director is telling you, which is inevitably something he hopes to make and not always something that he does make. Therefore one designs to the hype, and makes it bigger and more this and more that. It takes an extremely skilled director working in the commercial world to pull off a good product under those circumstances. Frightening!

I do think about the other elements of the theater: sound, costume. I was lighting a musical once. Often I pick color after I consider angle and equipment, but in this case the music was available and I was playing the tape. While I was listening, I took out the gel books and selected a bunch of colors that just seemed right; and then I got an envelope from the costume designer with a bunch of swatches, and what fell out of it were all the same colors. That's how I knew we were on the right track. That's what's fun about the theater: everyone's off working on their own, and then they come in and it's all the same colors, because we are getting it together. It's collaboration around the images—non-verbal or verbal, but non-specific comments that we all have at the beginning of a project.

Interpreting the clues

I feel my work is to support and reveal the art, in whatever circumstances we find ourselves. For me, it depends on figuring out what the art is in advance of it existing. I had a director who showed me a picture of a sand dune, a blue sky and a sand dune, that had ripples up it. And he said, "This is what I have in mind for *Twelfth Night*." Now, the scenic design had already been done, and it was a wall against a dark sky with a door, and in front of it was an extremely raked, textured floor with broken pieces of pianos all over it, so it was a conceptual place in which *Twelfth Night* would happen. The scenic designer and the director talked about wanting the moon, the stars, and the sky, and it was all dark blue and green and gray, and then he handed me this picture of a bright golden sand dune. Ha! I didn't say, "What is that?" I said, "Oh, how interesting, tell me more!" And it wasn't until I heard him talking to the scenic designer about the texture of the floor that I realized that what he liked about the sand dune image were the ripples, and what he was asking for were shin-busters and backlight to make sure that we saw the extremely textured floor. I do not expect a director to be able to communicate that clearly. If I've got somebody who can, great! But it's those kinds of clues that it's extremely important for a lighting designer to interpret.

Then of course, in addition to my own lighting ideas, I must take into account the context and the venue; if I've got a theater this big, where can I put lights? How many lights do they have? How many can I have? What's the quality of the crew? Are they inexperienced? Are they pros? How much work can we get done in a day? All of those factors go into the universe of the play. And it may be that the director is talking about the moon and the stars, which I would love to do with fiber optics and moving lights, but I cannot do that in a little university play. There is one sentence that I sometimes have to say: "Yes, I can do that, but your producers can't afford it." In fact sometimes a director will go to see a big show and say, "Why can't I … ?" He doesn't realize he's got the idea for something visual from a huge, expensive, commercial production, and now he wants to do it at La MaMa.

On compromise

Of course I can compromise and say, "With your budget I can do this …" It's rare that the request is for a specific kind of machine or an explicit look. It's easy to price that piece of equipment, and the producers can then yea or nay it. Your next responsibility as a designer is to offer other choices that are close to the specific idea, but less expensive.

An example would be that we're going to do a play, *Crocodile Eyes*, by Eduardo Machado, and the director wants a bonfire that looks as if it's a long way away. Well, I could get these machines with flames that wiggle, but they're very cartoon-like and I don't think that's appropriate. This is where I make my decision. I don't think it's

Twelfth Night, William Shakespeare. *University of Tennessee, Knoxville, Tennessee, USA, 2004. Directed by Blake Robeson. Moving lights hit the mylar walls to splash and shatter, creating the desired atmosphere for this production of* Twelfth Night.

Twelfth Night, William Shakespeare. *University of Tennessee, Knoxville, Tennessee, USA, 2004. Directed by Blake Robeson.*

appropriate to spend what little money I have on something that is going to look cartoon-like for Machado. So I go back to nature: the director has asked for night, but said he doesn't want it to be blue—well, that's correct, night isn't blue. So my next sentence is, "How do you want to see the actors?" Obviously, true night is black and he doesn't mean that, so are we talking about natural light sources and what would they be? One of them would be light coming from inside the house. And one of them might be, as he proposed, a bonfire. So if you imagine what it would be like to be lit up by a bonfire—it's really a dull red glow. Which may have a little motion in it. It's not literal flames, where you see lines on people's faces. So I'm not getting gizmos and gadgets to do that; I'm just going to have red and a glow.

I then visualize exactly what it would be like, if you were standing in a field at night and the fire were over there—one side of your face would have a reddish glow. So then I ask what equipment will do that and where can I put that equipment? The angle has to resemble a fire on the ground, so the red shouldn't be coming from over your head. That won't satisfy the eye.

Working with what is possible

I look for the logic of the play; the logic of the light sources that are there in nature. I work with what's possible in the situation, and I also know that there are certain givens. A director expects to see the actors' faces. It's a waste of all their time and a waste of the audience's money if they can't see them. If you can't see them, you can't hear them. So there are certain things we do: we make what's called "area light," ensuring that every part of the stage is covered with light from at least two angles, so that you can walk up and down the stage or back and forth without walking through dark spots. And we cover the entire space in that way. So any place on the stage where a director puts somebody, I've got light for them—not necessarily a pretty light, but at least it's a working light, so that the audience can see them.

Now in the case of the director who wants the play in the dark, how do I communicate night? He doesn't want any blue; he wants natural light sources. So you need to stretch the reality. You can start by saying that there's firelight from over there, so it's red. But now the actor needs to talk and to be seen. So I'll bring up that area light slightly below the brightness of this reddish glow, so that one half of his face is still reddish from below and the other half is filled in—just enough so that you can see him talk. And you've established what you want the audience to understand, and now you can see the actors talk because you've stated where you are and people comprehend it; and if you don't violate it, if I don't bring up those area lights too bright, the audience understands, "Okay, we're in that place, but there has been a theatrical adjustment so that I can just see. It feels dark, but there is enough light."

Lighting decisions

I go scene-by-scene, moment-by-moment, but I don't plan it in detail in advance. I physically lay out the area light—I don't know when I'm going to use it, but I know I'm going to. I lay out light coming from the high sides. I decide if it's the kind of piece that needs vertical or backlight.

Vertical (or downlight) is ugly: you see a bright nose, a hot forehead, but the eyes disappear. So it's not a light that the audience wants to see a character in by itself for very long. Are there any moments in this play that need that? Backlight might relate to sunlight, or it might not relate to anything—it just cuts people away from the background. So how much equipment do I have? Do I have enough to have some backlights and some downlights? Sometimes I don't have enough equipment, and I have to pick one sort of light. Is it the kind of a play that is full of dark caves and somber moments? How hard and brightly will backlight hit the floor? Is the whole space involved all the time, or has the director used the word "isolate"? Is it a play where I have to make places with no light leaks around the edges, or are they going to use all the space all the time?

Then there is the choreography. What is the visual necessity? If you've got a living-room scene, inevitably the whole room needs to be lit. But if you have a love scene, inevitably the director wants to take down all the light around the room and leave the sofa bright. But it shouldn't seem to go green over there—it must still be part of the same room; it's just a reduction in intensity. I have to hook up the light so that it will do that.

For me, much of the lighting design process is based on logic. But other people will say different things. And the motivational aspect of the piece is something that's non-verbal. Why I would pick a certain color over another color, I don't know; I just thought it might be interesting. What did I have available, for instance, for *Crocodile Eyes* when he said he didn't want blue? I had dark green. Blue is an artificial idea, so what other color might the night be? Might it be dark red? Yes, but we've got the dark red named as fire. So is there a way to fill the stage with a little backlight and a little edge that's not blue? So, dark green. I don't know whether the director's going to like it, whether it's going to resonate with him. I've got it there to offer. If I turn it on and he says, "What's that!" I know I don't need that color, and now I can change it to something else.

A palette of lighting choices

When I design a light plot, I think of the Renaissance painters and how they used to grind their colors. And when they put them blop-blop-blop on a palette, they'd already made some of their choices by picking those colors. They'd made a palette of colors and were thinking about them for that work. Even though they mixed them to get other colors, they had those colors to start with. I am making that palette of choices.

For me, a light plot is a palette of choices—angle, equipment, and color; choices that might work. And right away as I start to cue the show, I'm listening to see if the director likes or hates it, or if it's resonating with him, or if the color looks good on that dress. I didn't know about that dress till yesterday—oops, that color isn't going to work. I'm either working from this palette or I immediately say, "That one's no good, throw it away, and put another one there." So I stay flexible, but I do not design the moment in advance.

Tharon Musser, a famous lighting designer, said that the way she usually works is to take the climactic scene in a play and design that, then use what's essential for that moment as the key to the rest of the play, the plot. I can't do that. First of all, that moment hasn't been directed yet, so I can't see it. I'm not lighting a script, I am lighting two people standing and talking to each other in a space, wearing something against a set with furniture. This moment doesn't yet exist all together, so I can't visualize it. Should his face be bright because he's standing and looking this way? I don't know, they're not there, they haven't rehearsed, and nobody's set that blocking, so I can't have an opinion.

Dance—that's a different world. Before you make the plot, you're invited to see the finished piece. Here I can design in a very different way from how I can in the theater. I haven't done that much opera. Opera is more like theater, but with a greater limitation on time. They have wonderful equipment and crew possibilities, but because they do it in rep, time is very limited and the plots are standardized. The big opera houses have wonderful personnel—people who can put the focus back and maintain the look—but because they're in rep, you can't use tons of equipment the way you can for the commercial theater; there isn't time to refocus it. In a commercial show you focus it once and they then use it day after day. And that is it.

On lighting as a support

I don't think lighting gives the play movement and pushes it forward, but it does respond to the pace ... How the light is used punctuates and supports. I wouldn't say "pushes"; it supports the motion that the production needs.

Gypsy with Bernadette Peters was conceived as an old-fashioned piece. Somebody is singing a song at the end of a scene and the song is a familiar one, and everything turns blue and the scenery changes, and then you come up in a new scene. It has a slow and predictable pace. What Jules Fisher and Peggy Eisenhauer did with that problem, I thought was very interesting. They would take the lights out on the scenery while the star was still singing the song. We know it's over, the audience knows that scene is over, so they left the singer in a follow spot with a little pool of light around them and dumped out everything else, and people on stage started moving the scenery behind her.

The moment that song was over: iris down, bump out, bang in the blue [all technical descriptions of lighting cues] abruptly and, because they were using moving lights, they could do that with a cut and not a fade, and then bring the lights up immediately; they're in the next scene already. Great! Done fast and with tremendous energy, it kept the piece flowing forward instead of: sing a song, applause, stop, move the scenery, stop, come up in the next scene. They accelerated the musical and increased the excitement. But I don't think the word "pushing" is appropriate.

But if the director doesn't support that, you can't do it. Jules and Peggy couldn't have done that if the director hadn't had the confidence to move the scenery during the end of the song. "We'll take the lights out, you move the scenery." It's a collaboration. You are supporting the director's choice. And the director might say, "Is there any way to do this quicker?" And we might say, "Yeah, let her sing the song; let us get rid of the scene light." In other words, whoever's suggestion it was at that moment, it's based on a mutual idea: let's get the scenery moving, get that over with as quickly as possible. I contribute this idea, you contribute that.

I hope I'm a director's designer. I don't know how to do it any other way. Are there designers who say, "Leave me alone. I want to do it by myself"? Yes. And there are some directors who like that, who don't want as much input and say, "Just do it; just do it. I'm busy thinking about other things." I can do that. And I remain open if they come running back to me and say, "What is that?"

Aladdin, Alan Menken, Howard Ashman, and Tim Rice.
Children's Theatre of Minneapolis, Minneapolis, USA, 2005. Directed by Blake Robeson. A warm and welcoming scene at the beginning of this production of Aladdin.

A Midsummer Night's Dream, Benjamin Britten.
Chicago Opera Theater, USA, 2005. Directed by Andrei Serban. This production of the opera A Midsummer Night's Dream *featured a pink floor with a green grass carpet, yellow-shirted elves, and crystals tied to black ropes which filled the air. A 4K HMI diagonal back lighting was used.*

Einstein on the Beach, Philip Glass and Robert Wilson. *Brooklyn Academy of Music, Brooklyn, New York, USA, 1984. Directed by Robert Wilson. The1984 revival (original version staged in Avignon in 1976) of* Einstein on the Beach *(Trial, Act I, Scene 2). Note that each element has its own individual lighting treatment, and very little light hits the floor.*

On significant productions in terms of light

I've seen many significant productions. I worked with Tom Skelton on dance concerts, I worked with Jules Fisher on many kinds of productions. They were all different—all interesting. I worked with David Hersey and Chris Parry on projects that originated in the UK. Bob Wilson is interesting. Gerald Gutierrez's production of *The Heiress* was very successful, and people liked it.

A good design is one that doesn't stand apart from the production, one that doesn't assert itself. Now, if the production is about disco, you need "disco" lighting and that will be obvious lighting, but it still must not overpower and distract from the play itself. Telling the signatures of the different lighting designers is a non-verbal thing. Sometimes there are certain color choices that a person always makes. David Hersey always used up-to-date equipment in ways that other people hadn't yet.

Working with Robert Wilson

I worked for 13 years with Robert Wilson: *Einstein on the Beach* and *Civil Wars*, and all that. And he's the epitome of difficult, in the sense that he does want to do it all by himself and you are the brush in his hand. One of the things I'm proud of in my work with Wilson is that I kept teaching him what I was doing and how I was doing it. Partly so that he would quit asking for things that couldn't be done. And while you can't blame him for imagining things, you have to show him the reality. And if he's smart, he gets it. And he is very smart. He does get it. But in the intensity of his neediness, it has got to be done a certain way. Now!

I ended up collaborating with Bob because his piece *Letter to Queen Victoria* had toured Europe with a lighting assistant—now a fine lighting artist—called Carol Mullins. She had carefully noted what look Bob had liked in each cue of the show and how it was accomplished. Bob wanted to present the piece in a Broadway theater, which required a lighting designer who was a member of the United Scenic Artists (the designers' union). Mutual friends put us together.

One of the things I found interesting about Wilson is that in his own quiet way he'll hold up an entire production until the lighting's perfect. For instance, while some directors in the middle of the tech will say, "What's that splotch in the middle of the floor over there," they won't have time to let me find out the answer. They gallop on. With Wilson, it all stops. You go up on the stage and you discover that it's a little splash coming out of the side of that shutter; and you must fix it then.

I learned a tremendous amount working with Wilson, because he works to the limits of all the equipment, all the time, and to the limits of the patience of everyone involved. Nobody else will give you the kind of time that he insists he needs to light his pieces. And that was great. I loved that, because the entire opera house is standing and waiting while we say, "I think we should move it over a little." And we must get out the ladder and slide it over a bit right now, so that it is perfect. You don't get opportunities like that very often.

Because he breaks them, Bob reveals a lot of the unspoken rules by which we all live. One is that when you are a director, you agree that there will be something finished at eight o'clock when the audience turns up. Bob has never signed up for that. That's one of those unspoken theater things. No, he's like a visual artist—if it isn't perfect, he won't open it. That's going by his standards; it may not be my opinion of perfect, but it's his opinion.

I'm not talking about perfect in terms of aesthetics; I'm talking about perfect in what you're trying to do. And with Wilson what you're trying to do is always out at the extremes. He tries to accomplish clear lighting ideas that are technically very difficult. One of the interesting things about Bob is that you cannot say, "You can't do that, it can't be done." As theater designers, we are

all trained to recommend to a director, "This isn't a good idea. It's not likely to happen; it's going to be a mess every time; it's not worth it." Bob demands 100 percent. Knowing what will happen, I should make him quit at 40 percent of what he wants. But because that's not possible, he gets 80 percent of what he is looking for—astounding! But he's unhappy, still hoping for that 100 percent. The fact that we're getting 80 percent of all the things he wants, I think that's pretty good. And that spirit presses everyone to do something extraordinary. Sometimes he comes up with interesting solutions.

All directors decide which battles are worth fighting. Bob will go to the mat for the way he wants it to look. If the management company is slow, or dragging its heels, or lying to him about what it is willing to provide, he slows down the lighting rehearsal—and lo and behold, it isn't finished. So it doesn't open on the official opening night. Bob has taken the gamble that it will be more important to do that piece right than to be invited back.

Liviu might make a different choice. It's more important for him to be invited back and to do something that's acceptable to the producers than it is for Bob. And it's the job of the producer to evaluate the artists they want: their working style and the quality of the finished product. Wilson now knows how to light a stage. When I first started working with him, he knew a lot less. There were other designers who had worked with him before me, but they had had a rough time. He knows how to handle himself—if he chooses not to, that's his choice. He's a fabulous guy. And the things he's accomplished over the years and the work he's done are just extraordinary.

Training

I was a dancer in college and I was interested in the process of taking work that had been made in a sheltered, quiet rehearsal studio and putting it on the stage—and the great hullabaloo of equipment, crew, and schedules. I was interested in how we protect the work and its integrity, and how we show it to an audience without getting everyone's nerves shattered. I didn't know lighting design existed. I was interested in stage management and the planning aspect of it, and then lighting came along as something I was curious about. I just started doing it.

You don't do it by yourself. I assisted Tom Skelton, during college in the early Sixties. And then I got hired by Merce Cunningham to do lighting for his company. I did lighting for Meredith Monk at the beginning of her career. People would invite me to light their show. So I just lit them, and at the same time I assisted Tom and Jules Fisher, who got me into the commercial world. And of course Jules would have a show go out on the road, and I would get it going on the road. So I developed the vocabulary to work in the commercial world as well as the regionals, the not-for-profits, the art stuff.

I think the Brooklyn Academy of Music stage is a beautiful proscenium stage. I like big, beautiful stages. Even for small works, I like a big, beautiful stage. City Center is a beautiful, big theater; it puts the dancers in your lap. I have worked at Arena Stage in Washington, but arenas cut your choice of angles. The viewers are all around and you have less control over how it looks.

Advice for someone going into theater

Be open to the possible. I remember Jules Fisher saying to some director who was afraid to articulate what he wanted, "Just say what you want. Men have been to the Moon, you know." We might not be able to do it, but we certainly can't do it if you don't say what you're imagining, because you might imagine it's this big. It's all about what lands emotionally for the audience. If you want Niagara Falls, you've got to go make a movie. As soon as you're in the theater you can't have Niagara Falls precisely. But what is it about Niagara Falls that you're after: the thundering intensity of it, the vertical motion? In the theater that's what we're about—we're after essence.

A palette of possibilities

We all have our personal methods of approaching a job. As I read the play, and when I see the set designer's work, if I see a pretty pink living room, I'm not going to light it all green with vast shafts of light. That's a violation of the play. I just know by looking at it. Often I can explain it after the fact, after we've cued it, tried it: "Well, I had that big shaft, but it didn't work for this and that reason, so we evolved something else." But to walk in with a finished idea about what we should have is not my way of working, and I don't think most designers work that way. They may tell you differently, but they don't.

I don't design beforehand. I design a palette of possibilities—of things to try—and then we find out how it fits. And often that varies from play to play, from theater to theater. And for me it's still a very exciting adventure.

Biography

Beverly Emmons has designed lighting for Broadway, off-Broadway, and regional theater, dance, and opera, both in the US and abroad. Her Broadway credits include *Annie Get Your Gun, Jekyll & Hyde, The Heiress, Chronicle of a Death Foretold, Stephen Sondheim's Passion, Abe Lincoln in Illinois, High Rollers, Stepping Out, The Elephant Man, A Day in Hollywood, A Night in the Ukraine, The Dresser, Piaf,* and *Doonesbury.* Her lighting of *Amadeus* won a Tony Award. At the Welsh National Opera she designed *Cosi Fan Tutti* for Liviu Ciulei and *Rigoletto* for Lucian Pintilie. In the regional theaters she has worked many times at the Guthrie, Arena Stage, ART, and the Children's Theatre of Minneapolis. Off-Broadway she lit *Vagina Monologues* and has designed numerous productions with Joseph Chaikin and Meredith Monk. For Robert Wilson she has designed lighting for productions spanning 13 years; most notably, in America, *Einstein on the Beach* and the *Civil Wars Pt V.* Emmons' designs for dance have included works for the companies of Martha Graham, Trisha Brown, Alvin Ailey, and Merce Cunningham. She has been awarded seven Tony nominations, the 1976 Lumen Award, 1984 and 1986 Bessies, a 1980 Obie for Distinguished Lighting, and several Maharam/ American Theatre Wing Design Awards.

Susan
Hilferty
Costume
Design

A close collaborator of Athol Fugard and a designer of Broadway and off-Broadway productions, as well as the chair of the design department at Tisch School of the Arts, Susan Hilferty discusses the importance of dramaturgy in the design process. For her, design is not really possible without paying close attention to details and uncovering them as a professional dramaturg would. She also discusses costume design in relation to other design elements, such as set and lighting design, and how and why they are ultimately related.

Too Clever by Half, Alexander Ostrovsky.

Guthrie Theater, Minneapolis, USA, 1994. Directed by Garland Wright. An actor living in a graphic space is defined by silhouette. In this case, the choices include glasses, hair, teeth, and the size of a pattern in the fabric, all of which help the actor match the scale of the scenery, and allow the performer to resonate in space.

Introduction

In this interview Susan Hilferty explains how "Every single show I do starts from a different place." But regardless of its starting point, they are all a response to the text. "Being a theater designer, the text could be a piece of music, a piece of choreography, a play—but the text is the trigger." Hilferty illustrates this using the example of *Hamlet*, where she does a close reading of the play. "What the designer is doing," she explains, "is creating a world, and the audience is looking through a window and observing specific elements of that world." To this end, all choices need to be precise and clearly thought out.

Speaking about costume design, she says, "There's no such thing as a good costume design separated from a good production." The two go hand in hand, and costumes cannot stand alone. She also gives insights into the theater world today, as well as commenting on the student training at the New York University's Tisch School of the Arts.

"I almost always begin the exploration of a play in my head in the time that it's written."

Approach

For me, designing the costumes always starts with the text. And I approach each play differently, so I wait for the script to give me, not information, but inspiration. Everything I do is in response to a text. Being a theater designer, the text could be a piece of music, a piece of choreography, a play—but the text is the trigger. I always start there. I think all designers do. I think that is the secret.

What the designer is doing is creating a world, and the audience is looking through a window and observing specific elements of that world—they only see and know very specific things: particular actors in relationship to that scenery, lit in that way, saying those lines. I am talking here about the four dimensions. We deal with the three dimensions of a space—a living space—but we also deal with time and silences. For me, the trigger to almost every design: the timing, the rhythm; trying to understand what that rhythm is, and then including silences—great moments of silence used correctly, like punctuation in the course of story-telling. I use the timing, or rhythm, to begin to establish the essential nature of the world. I also usually include in my thinking a sense of light: what its qualities are, what the qualities of the space and time of day or mood are.

Designing *Hamlet*

I have always wanted to design *Hamlet. Hamlet* takes place in a very brief time period. It almost feels as if it's happening in a day. You're looking at a really tightly driven machine that's moving inexorably until the final moment, the death of Hamlet. For me, it has a sense of movement, a sense of drive. You'll see this even in the ghost scene, as it moves from place to place. And you get the sense that *Hamlet* has an increasing energy. That's important for me in terms of what the world is like. And who is occupying that world.

Light is one of the other ingredients that I use to try to understand what the design elements are about. If you look through *Hamlet*, there are outside scenes. Everybody imagines that they know where Ophelia has drowned, but we're actually not out there when it happens. As the scene begins there's the sense, in my head, that almost all takes place in darkness. Then you have the scenes inside. These would be some of the thoughts that I would bring to the first meeting with the director.

My next step in trying to define the world would be—and this is always a complicated issue for a costume designer—trying to define a period or a time. I almost always begin the exploration of a play in my head in the time that it's written. I never look to find another period that it might fit.

Too Clever by Half, Alexander Ostrovsky.

Guthrie Theater, Minneapolis, USA, 1994. Directed by Garland Wright. Each of the actors has been physically altered in this production. Corseting, padding, dental work, wigs, and prosthetics are combined with the actor's skill at defining their physical gesture to create a character.

GORC ULIN

MAMAEV

I'm more interested in what the space feels like. Is it about movement? I look for signals other than just another time period to help me identify the placement of the clothes.

Hamlet is also one of those plays that's really driven by one character, seen through his eyes. To me, that becomes an important element: that you have somebody who is a prince, plus a king and a queen, so the culture of this world has to have a "kingness." There also has to be a place where we understand the crown will be handed over, and there's a weight to this crown. Those elements start to come into my sense of what that world is. I would never want to begin a production with the thought that I knew Hamlet was mad, or not mad. I think that's really the journey the actor takes, and ultimately it's a secret that the actor has, so you don't feel that you're *solving* a play. I always believe that you're exploring a play each time, instead of solving it. *Hamlet* is such an interesting play because, for the actor playing the role, so much happens before he even comes on. Even the first entrance is critical: when he comes on, does he move off? Does he just creep on? Is he on stage all the time and then suddenly appears?

Once I've established that there's going to be a monarchy, that gives me the essence of the place. I would include whether or not there's a lot of talk in *Hamlet* about war. That would be one of the major elements that I would explore. Fortinbras [the Prince of Norway] is coming through: what is that about, and what is the sense of place? Is it somewhere war is present, and so everybody is armed and ready in some way? Has the new king given an easygoing, casual air to the court since the death of the older king?

One of the interesting questions is what costume the ghost appears in. They talk about him wearing some sort of uniform, or his armor from a previous battle. Those are things that I would try to weigh up, in terms of understanding the quality of Elsinore.

Translating text to design

Translating thought into a design is the hard part. If we make the decision that this is a world where Hamlet has a sense of paranoia, but there's real tension in the court caused by everybody being nervous about losing their head or job, I could start to use that. I probably wouldn't go so far as to say that I'm going to make it like Hitler's Germany. I wouldn't necessarily use that as a specific reference, but I would start weighing up the qualities of different cultures and places that give me access to that kind of paranoia. Stalin is another example.

Too Clever by Half, Alexander Ostrovsky.

Guthrie Theater, Minneapolis, USA, 1994. Directed by Garland Wright. Through the sketch the designer can explore proportion, character, and color. Decisions in the fitting room start with the impulse expressed in the drawing as the two-dimensional thought is turned into a three-dimensional reality.

Too Clever by Half, Alexander Ostrovsky.

Guthrie Theater, Minneapolis, USA, 1994. Directed by Garland Wright. The shape of the belly, the height of the collar, and the color of the hair are all decisions that can be explored in the sketch. Mamaev should appear as though he could be blown away like a helium balloon.

060

The Seagull, Anton Chekhov.

Guthrie Theater, Minneapolis, USA, 1993. Directed by Garland Wright. The world of Chekhov's Seagull *is seen through the filter of dreams in this production. Arkadina, the consumate actress, performs her life in the country far from the world she dreams about. The bottle green of her dress pulls her from the stain of country life.*

"I believe that every designer has to think holistically."

I have to help make directorial choices. I work with the actors—I'm the one who's working most closely with them as they create a character. I have to be privy to their journey from the mundane to the complicated, in order to be able to help them arrive at a character.

These are certainly questions the dramaturg should ask, but if the costume designer doesn't also ask them, they aren't getting at a world. Having the dramaturg know information like that, and not putting it at the heart of what the designer is doing, means that the design has no connection. I'm only interested in finding ways to make that world a living place occupied by these specific actors saying these specific words.

The role of the costume designer

The costume designer's job is very complicated, because not only do you have to know (which is a whole job in itself) how to design clothes, color, fabric, and construction, but also the second part is to understand real history so that you can identify what you would do in 1776. Then the third part is to take all that information and abstract it, so that it's not a specific time or place. You have to have the skill to extract a design idea. Designers have to know about history and its relationship to the world, whether it's about the sciences, war, or politics; we have to know about literature, because almost every great play references other great plays. When we do Brecht, we have to know Shakespeare—they are referencing each other and we must understand the context. We have to be so close to the actor's journey that we get to see the actor in both lives. I have to deal with an actor who has problem feet and a bad stomach, and insecurities about weight and baldness, but then I'm the one who has to take that actor through the transformation to become somebody else. Actors have to trust that I will not make them look bad. At the same time I have to be confident enough in my choices that I can take them to the place they need to be. It's the greatest compliment when they're finally dressed and say, "Now I know who I am." Because then I know that I've melded all those pieces.

Drawing the costumes

I constantly put pen to paper—from the very beginning I draw. Just as an actor is trying things from the moment they read the role—it might be with an accent, or in the way they move—so a costume designer has to try things out. If my initial impulse with *Hamlet* is the sense that it's inexorably driven, as a set designer I start to have a sense of what the transitions are and how movement affects the story.

Every single show I do starts from a different place. I'm not only dealing with different plays, but also with different directors. The impulse always comes from a different place—it's always a surprise. There's a great Southern expression, "Well, shut my mouth," for that magic moment when you know that you have somehow combined all of these things into the design. You'll do something and then your job is to respond to your own work. To be constantly questioning and trying to understand what the impulse is, so that you do it and say, "That's what I thought, but what is wrong or right with this choice?"

I believe that every designer has to think holistically. If I put somebody in black in a white space, that's one thing; if I put someone in black in a black space, that's a completely different thing; if I put someone in black in a black space with a bright light on them, that's another thing; if I put them in candlelight, that's something else. So you have to keep thinking about the universe, and the manners and mores of the universe and how they affect each other.

Working with directors

There is no set route for what I talk about with a director. When I did all my work with Garland Wright, he almost always began our conversations with what the play sounded like. He was never specific about visuals. For him, it was "This is the music that I hear in relationship to this play." And that was always the stepping stone to where the design would go. You just never knew where it was going to lead. But his sound ideas released my imagination, taking with it all my other senses of what the play was about. As soon as I knew what he was hearing, I could start to imagine the bits and pieces of that world. I never think, "Oh I'm going to set it in 1777."

I had a great teacher, Tom Skelton, the lighting designer. He would say, "You should always keep your ideas relative." Instead of saying, "I want it to be red," you say, "I want it to be warmer than that" or "I want it to be cooler than that." Then, instead of it having to be red, which is so specific as an idea, you know that you want to make it hot—so you can make green hot, you can make purple hot. You come out of it in a different way, depending on the space. I would never go into a meeting saying, "It has to be set in the Twenties." I wouldn't even know how to get there. I would come with questions or answers, too.

I'm one of the luckiest people I know. I've worked with the greatest directors in the world. I've had an unbelievable list of experiences, and almost every one has been rich and fantastic. And never—or very rarely, because I never work with that person again—do I have a director who either gives me nothing to play with or is dictatorial. I call myself a not-for-profit baby, because that's where I grew up.

I did all of Athol Fugard's plays for the last 20 years. You can't beat an experience like that. I've been working with Richard Nelson doing costumes and now scenery for the last six years. I've done all his plays since he started directing his own. And working with Garland Wright at the Guthrie for over a decade was pivotal in my work. I'm extremely lucky.

On time and character

One of the things that's astonishing to me about the theater is how compact a form of storytelling it is. If you go to a party and you're there for two hours, and you've met a lot of people and you think, "Can I remember the names of all 20 people I have met? Do I remember their stories?" But when you go to a play, to *Hamlet*, it's three hours long and you know everything about this person: you know their lineage, their history, their deepest, darkest thoughts, their experiences. You know that about 20 people. What's happening on stage is this intense experience that you, as an audience member, are part of. Without being aware of the mechanics—without noticing—you have hopefully been guided through it. Because everybody has been working on the same journey. Not only the designers, but also the director and each of the actors. That's why I say that time is one of the essential ingredients to being a designer, and especially a costume designer, because you are there framing a journey from beginning to end.

Sometimes you can do something huge with a character. Take *Wicked*, because it's simple storytelling without a lot of loops in the story. I've got one character who is a kind of ditzy, sweet woman, and by the end she's a power-hungry killer. I used pictures of Queen Elizabeth I, moving her from this innocent woman to somebody who's got her hair scraped back, structured and powerful. Some-times you get to tell the story that way.

Wicked, Stephen Schwartz and Winnie Holzman.
Gershwin Theater, New York, USA, 2004. Directed by Joe Mantello. Designing Wicked *required the creation of a universe rooted in the turn of the century when the* Wizard of Oz *was written, but seen through a contemporary eye; twisted Edwardian. This silhouette was inspired by the bustle and then balanced with a "boot" hat.*

Wicked, Stephen Schwartz and Winnie Holzman.
Gershwin Theater, New York, USA, 2004. Directed by Joe Mantello. Asymmetrical, off kilter, but charged with a sense of style, the residents of the city wear green glasses to enhance their signature color. Green fur and feathers are de rigeur.

"There's no such thing as good costume design separated from a good production."

On good design

There is no such thing as good costume design separated from a good production. You can't have good costumes and a bad production. It's not possible—that's what I say. As a costume designer, you don't get credit for a great performance, but rarely do you have a great performance with a terrible costume. It's been done, but I really believe that it's got to feel as if it's all coming from the same place.

The most influential production I ever saw wasn't a single production. I'd come from a small town in Massachusetts, and I was an actress. I chose to go to Syracuse University, where I was in the arts school and I minored in fashion design. I was learning how to make clothes and understand them, but I was also painting. And I was doing my work study in the student theater. I worked as a scenic artist and in all the different shops. But at that point I had never really seen any professional theater. Then I did my semester abroad. I'd never traveled at all—never been to New York City. I was really connected to what people called Conceptual Art, like Laurie Anderson, Claus Oldenberg. All of that work, including the performance work, was influential on my thinking, even though I was (and continue to be) influenced by painting. And then I went to London, and once a week, or sometimes twice a week, I saw professional shows. That whole body of work is what influenced me to become a theater designer. I saw the original production of *Equus*, a really beautiful Peter Schaeffer play. John Napier, who did *Cats*, designed the set. It was very, very simple—very smart. I saw the original production of the *Rocky Horror Show*, which was in cabaret: turning on a fluorescent light to create lightning. I began to understand what theater design was.

And I kept a diary, and as I watched more, I thought, "Oh! Oh! Oh!" It was eye-opening. I understood what the process of design was. I understood what directing was about. I came back to New York and knew I was going to be a designer. I teach costumes at NYU, as well as being the chairman. So I deal with all aspects of design. I'm much more fluent in the specifics of the craft of being a costume designer than a set designer. But in terms of the conceptual thinking, I'm both.

Teaching at NYU

I started teaching at NYU in 1992, and I think this is my seventh year as chair. I wish there was a specific teaching strategy. I have written mission statements identifying our goals. I'm lucky because I've got great colleagues like John Conklin. John is basically what I would call the dramaturg of the department. We spend a lot of time connecting text to students' work. At the same time students have to develop as visual artists, so we try to braid together all these threads, so that they can under-stand how to make connections like an artist. One thread is understanding the technique—whether it's stagecraft or model making or drawing. The other part is how we all work as collaborators: what happens in the rehearsal room, in the cauldron; the place where it really matters.

School is a place where we ask students questions. What happens? What is the event? And you can constantly ask students really hard questions in terms of their work. Of course, some will understand the experience better than others. Some will get it, and others will wrestle with it and not necessarily understand how to put it together. Since you're dealing with an art form, you can only keep asking questions, but you can't make somebody think in a certain way. You can't say, "This is the way to do it." But I can guide them and say, "These may be paths for you to follow."

Wicked, Stephen Schwartz and Winnie Holzman.

Gershwin Theater, New York, USA, 2004. Directed by Joe Mantello. The Mob is chasing after the Wicked Witch in their overcoat-based designs. Distorted with hip and shoulder pads, they feel threatening. Hats pulled down and collars pulled up help disguise their identity.

Jitney, August Wilson.

Mark Taper Forum, LA, USA, 2000; Second Stage, New York, and Off Broadway, New York, USA, 2001. Directed by Marion McClinton. August Wilson's Jitney *focuses on a segment of life in The Hill District of Pittsburgh. Though set in the Seventies, emotionally, the men occupy the years following World War II. The life of Fielding, once a master tailor, is reflected in his suit, carefully maintained and mended through his years of drinking.*

Theater versus opera

I prefer theater to opera. That's where my heart has been, because I really believe in theater's connection to a community. I loved working at the Guthrie, because I knew I was connecting with a whole community in Minnesota. And when I worked in San Francisco, at each of those places I really felt as if I was a part of a community and doing work within it.

Broadway has different values. These days, it's so complicated to produce on Broadway that you're constantly struggling with confused values. I have just done a huge commercial hit, so I can't be critical of it. It's unbelievable what happened to *Wicked*: it's taken off as a production, and there's something really interesting about having a huge success. *Rodney's Wife*, Richard Nelson's play, was being compared to great plays, it was a great production, but it finished its run and is gone. I've always been able to live with that. But it's also interesting to have something that's running and running.

Now, in another year or so I might get really bored with it. There are always things that are vestigial—that, when you did it the first time, needed to be fixed. As a designer I work with actors, and there are new actors all the time. So I'm constantly going in. It would be easy to put them in the same clothes as the person before them wore. But new actors are doing it, they're different: different emotionally, and different physically, and I must work with the differences.

The *Wicked* story is an interesting one. When I first joined, I did so for two reasons: the story; and Joe Mantello, the director. I am a director-designer. When people ask me, "What kind of play do you want to work on?" I wouldn't want to do *Hamlet* just for *Hamlet's* sake; but if Joe Mantello directed *Hamlet*, then I would want to work with him. And the money—well, it's fantastic to be able to spend enough to realize your designs.

As a not-for-profit theater artist, what I think is a crime is the lack of funding. For the NEA [National Endowment for the Arts]. I don't see what happens in financing commercial plays. But the NEA, and the fact that the budgets have been cut back, that's a crime. Not recognizing that the essence of any culture is the arts, and that at this moment—when we are at war and at a crisis moment in terms of our time—silencing the inquisitors and those who are asking questions, that's a crime.

Personal opinions

Joe Mantello is directing *Glengarry Glenn Ross*, and many people would say, "That's just a bunch of shirts and ties, so why would you want to do it?" But I would love to do it—those characters are so complex. And I'll do anything that Richard Nelson does. I'll do anything that Athol Fugard does. These are incredible craftsmen; you know that you are in good hands. You're going on a complex journey, but you're not going to be abandoned somewhere in the middle of it.

On reading

The Internet is a complicated tool, but an important one. I learn so much by just browsing through books. On the Internet you can't truly browse. I've always been a reader—a close reader. I spend as much time as I can reading. You become obsessed. You have to become obsessed.

Reading critically is a learned experience. I send a reading list to all students before they come to classes. It used to be a long list of about 200 plays, but I have shortened the list to about 15. Before classes begin, the incoming students spend a session with John Conklin and myself asking questions about plays on the reading list. And that leads to a long conversation. For instance, "In what text is this important prop: a purple flower?" Immediately somebody gets it, so we look at *Midsummer Night's Dream.* You have to design the purple flower. What's its importance? Why purple? What does it represent? This may lead to other questions. Is this a place of sexuality? What is the purple flower?

It's a great experience for the students, because we make it clear before they even start classes that they are going to be close readers. And that they will design based on the text. They aren't allowed in class without the text in their hands.

One of the things that's exciting about teaching is that you have to keep challenging yourself about what it is that you're trying to teach. I believe that a young designer needs a balance in their classes between design, drawing, painting, craft, production, and dramaturgy. A designer must be skilled in all of these areas.

Biography

Susan Hilferty is a designer of opera, film, television, and dance, and has designed more than 200 productions for theaters across America. Internationally, her work has been produced in London, South Africa, Canada, and Australia. Recent credits include Broadway productions of *Into the Woods* (Tony nomination and Hewes Award), *Jitney*, *Wicked*, and *Dirty Blonde*; *Moby Dick*, Laurie Anderson; *Good Night Children Everywhere*, Richard Nelson, Playwrights' Horizons; *Chesapeake*, Lee Blessing, off-Broadway; director, *Sorrows and Rejoicings*, Athol Fugard, McCarter Theatre, Spoleto Festival, South Africa, Second Stage; director, *Valley Song*, Athol Fugard; *How to Succeed in Business Without Really Trying*, Broadway and national tour. She has designed 20 productions for Athol Fugard and is currently working with him as co-director and designer. She chairs the Department of Design for Stage/Film at New York University's Tisch School of the Arts. Her numerous awards include a 2004 Tony, and the Drama Desk and Outer Critics Circle Awards for *Wicked*.

Constance
Hoffman
Costume
Design

If the theater and opera are, by definition, collaborative arts, this collaboration is best illustrated by costume designer Constance Hoffman, when she discusses her work and collaboration on Shakespeare's *A Midsummer Night's Dream.* The design process, she points out, begins with reading the text, meditating on it, and pulling out images to start working with. The genesis of the collaboration starts with the first meeting with other designers and the director, where the whole team gets together for the first time and generates ideas for the production.

Introduction

A Midsummer Night's Dream, William Shakespeare. *Shakespeare Theatre, Washington DC, USA, 2003. Directed by Mark Lamos.*

In her interview Constance Hoffman reveals a quintessential aspect of the theater and opera—namely, that of collaboration. Yet prior to the first meeting of all the designers and directors, there is still work to be done. "I highlight the text, and I pull passages out." This is the first step, where "I just keep it very loose." During this stage, if any images come to mind, she draws them. She also gathers materials to feed her first impressions and clarify them.

Then the first meeting occurs. At the first meeting for a production of *A Midsummer Night's Dream,* her focus was on the minor character of the Indian boy and, through sketching and designing the costumes for this character, Hoffman unveiled the costumes for all the other major characters.

A Midsummer Night's Dream, William Shakespeare. *Shakespeare Theatre, Washington DC, USA, 2003. Directed by Mark Lamos.*

A Midsummer Night's Dream, William Shakespeare. *Shakespeare Theatre, Washington DC, USA, 2003. Directed by Mark Lamos.*

"I like to start at that pure place just with the text, without any input, and simply let it talk to me."

Approach

It seems kind of obvious, but I start with the text. No matter what the nature of the project is, that's where I begin and what I use as a touchstone and a resource for everything that the design becomes. Obviously I read the text, but I also meditate on it and pull things out of it during that meditation that help me, give me images to start with, impressions to begin with, things that intrigue me about it. That's work that I generally do before I ever meet the director. I'll obviously know who I'm going to be working with, and we may have had a brief conversation about where we need to go, and what that director's interested in; or we may not—it depends on who it is. But I like to start at that pure place just with the text, without any input, and simply let it talk to me. I've done several plays a number of times, and I find that they don't need to be designed the same way twice. Each time I work on it, it speaks to me in a different way. I did *Midsummer Night's Dream* a couple of times ... The two designs are completely different from one another.

I will be looking at different aspects of the text. I guess they're different because of what happens in my head, and in my life and my emotional state, and certainly in the world. I think that probably has the most effect. As I read a text, I start relating it to the world, I begin thinking about what's going on now, and how that text speaks to the world we're in. I think that's probably what leads me the most. It may not be that we're doing a contemporary production of the play, but certain events or dynamics or feelings in the air are going to make me pay attention in a different way to different things in each approach, so I think that's really where it starts.

I write my first impressions down, I highlight the text, and I pull passages out. Examples I can think of right now are of Shakespeare, but I do the same thing when I do an opera. I'll pull out parts of the text and often write them on the bottom of the page. The first read—particularly if I've never read or done a piece before—is just to experience it. And I don't work very hard at making connections; I just let it go through me, I just absorb it. And then I sit down again, with a different kind of attention—a more analytical attention. And that's when I start to take notes and write down some thoughts, and I just keep it very loose. Sometimes an image will jump into my head, and I'll draw something. But it's usually not quite ready to happen. I need to let it simmer for longer.

A Midsummer Night's Dream, William Shakespeare. *Shakespeare Theatre, Washington DC, USA, 2003. Directed by Mark Lamos.*

A Midsummer Night's Dream, William Shakespeare. *Shakespeare Theatre, Washington DC, USA, 2003. Directed by Mark Lamos.*

Research

At this point I would start to gather and/or make images. Go out, look through some of the books that I have, if I think I have something that feels like what this is. I might start working the assistant who's going to do the research, and say, "I'm looking for these kinds of images." But usually this is still personal work at this point.

I might run around in bookstores, I might go to museums. It depends on what I feel is coming up—what approach. Is it historical? Is it completely fantastical? Is it a more contemporary feeling? Am I even ready to say what those quotes actually are? Often I'm not. I'll just start to gather things: stuff that feeds my impressions, helps to clarify my first impressions, starts to approach some kind of concept, something concrete. And that's usually when I meet the director. Ideally we're all coming to the table having done that, and we're meeting the set designer, the light designer. And those are the best sorts of meetings.

I usually come to that first meeting either with a binder full of images or a stack of books. When I'm working at long distance, I tend to be more compact and put things together in a more presentational way. Usually by this time I've also done the necessary drudgery, which is a costume breakdown. And that is a totally necessary exercise, which actually helps on the subconscious work, because it's a way of working out who's in what scene and writing it down on paper in an organized way. It cements the given dramaturgy of a piece in my mind. At the same time as I want just to dream at this point, I also have to know structurally what the story needs to be, who's on stage and what they're doing, and what the parameters of the text suggest. And I think that's really a useful thing for a costume designer; it's a useful thing for any designer.

What I find with designing is that I can never get too far away from keeping track of the practical part of who's doing what where. So a third reading is useful to enable me to bring that knowledge to the director. The director is also doing that work, of course. But it's good for us to be at that point together, so that we don't get carried away and tell a story that isn't there. That's a nice anchor. You can always just go back to that and say, "That's a great idea, now let's see where these people really are, and what this scene is about ..." Then we all sit and share our impressions about this piece.

Sometimes sketches start to come at that first meeting. The reason I don't really get to sketches at that point is partly because I want to stay completely open to what my collaborators are bringing to the table. I don't want to start narrowing the field and saying, "This is what this is" until we've all had a chance to say what we feel it is, mutually. I want to be as open to and affected by things they bring to the table as I am by the things that I've brought myself. I might have done some drawings, but I might not even be ready to show them until I hear what everybody else has on their minds. Maybe somebody has this brilliant image that guides the whole production to a new place. At that stage of the game I think it's really important to stay open—to be receptive, but to come to the table with a lot to offer as well.

I'm thinking of the *Midsummer Night's Dream* that I did in Washington, DC at the Shakespeare Theatre. That first meeting was a really good example of what I'm talking about. I had a lot of books around, but I also had my whole library. We kept coming back to the Indian boy who is mentioned in the text, but doesn't necessarily ever reappear. We had each pondered what this character was about. The conversation kept cycling back to it. And we'd also talked a lot about what Mark Lamos [the director] was feeling; we knew that we were being asked to do

C.D. 96
COSTUME
SIGNATURE

TITANIA
C.D. 962
COSTUME DESIGNER
SIGNATURE

TITANIA
C.D. 96
COSTUME DESIG
SIGNATURE

OBERON

C.D. 962
COSTUME DESIGNER
SIGNATURE

"After we sit with these images that we've gathered and talked about, and come up with an approach that we all feel excited by, that's the impetus for drawing."

a production in which there was flying, which might not necessarily have been Mark's choice, but Shakespeare had wanted to put on stage a *Midsummer Night's Dream* that had flying. So we were talking about flying, we were talking about the fairies—which fairies would fly, and what fairies are.

And two ideas came up. The Indian boy idea kept shifting in and out of the conversation, and the idea that the fairies were like workers. And I thought of a book that I had with photographs that were all self-portraits of this man in a sad little business suit, in these tableaux that the photographer had set up about large, out-of-scale parts of the world. Simple, melancholy images about the Earth and man's place in it. And so I brought that book to the table, and suddenly Mark responded to that as a kind of feeling for the world. So that affected the set design, and it affected the look of the fairies. That all the things that made the fairies—their wings, their strange shapes—were things these men had gathered and tied around them, and were all very childlike and handmade. And the childlike quality started moving us back to the boy. And by the end of the conversation, the Indian boy was a central character in our production.

The boy was basically adopted, as a product of that world, an orphan of the war they had just fought. And his dream is really sorting out his new position in the world, and what these parents are—if they're parents, if they love each other, if they'll be comforting to him. And the dream is his dealing with the war and the stresses of parenthood, and being a child and all those things. And the fairies were then his creations. So all of that evolved out of this dialogue in which I brought a book to the table and the set designer responded. I wouldn't have known what to draw yet, until we'd had a conversation like that in which we sorted out what we were going to say.

Sometimes it takes two or three meetings before we know what we're going to end up doing. But generally after that first meeting we may have decided to go in a direction for which I have no images and need to do a lot of new research. In which case, that will happen next and we'll probably have an intermediate meeting, where people can look at that research and see if it's heading in the right direction. And it might be after that that I start sketching. In general, after we sit with these images that we've gathered and talked about, and come up with an approach that we all feel excited by, that's the impetus for drawing. That's when I imagine a world for the play to live in, a world in which to design, and I start drawing.

A Midsummer Night's Dream, William Shakespeare.
Shakespeare Theatre, Washington DC, USA, 2003. Directed by Mark Lamos. Drawings for costume designs. Titania and Oberon in two scales: as giant adversaries and as vulnerable intimates.

"I think costumes have an enormous effect on the performer and on the whole stage picture."

Costume design and color

When I begin to draw, that happens in stages too. I tend to go back and read through the script again. I think writing helps to focus me, in a way; it helps me get ready to draw. It's not always the way that I get into it, but sometimes I have to go through a discipline of some sort to cover the whole world. I certainly think there are as many ways of approaching that as there are designers. I go back to my breakdown and look at the whole picture, which is sitting there in verbal form for me at that point. I'll often take notes, just writing whether we've decided it's an 18th-century feeling, but may not be completely historical; or I might go through the whole character breakdown, and just write to myself what's going on in this scene. I often take notes about the arc of a character on that breakdown. Then I can keep it next to me while I'm sorting through images. Throughout this process I've also been sorting through images and narrowing down characters. That's something I'm doing constantly during the research—shaping and focusing it so that, when I'm ready to draw, I have things that help me focus on what my impulses are. It's a sort of dialogue with myself—dreaming about what this world is and what the characters are about, and then disciplining that work into a structure, always refining it as I'm going through the drawing process.

As for choosing the colors, the forest [in a *Midsummer Night's Dream*] was very clear to us, in that it was the color of dried leaves. So you already have one strong context. The Athenian court had colder, darker colors in the beginning. The set changed slightly, but it was always the same palette. The color palette of Athens was not terribly different from the forest.

I took my cue from the photos in the book that I shared in that first meeting. Those were all sepia-toned photos, and they informed the whole world. We looked at the man in the context of the space, and we felt that was a good thing, a good balance. So we knew that we wanted the fairies to be in sepia tones, and the scenery to be in sepia tones. And then the denizens of Athens were in darker colors, particularly if you're thinking from the perspective of this boy: how these adults were big, looming, somewhat scary people. It felt right that they would be dark, and would seem severe to him. Another thing Mark was interested in—and I think it governed a lot of his responses—was that he was looking at Puck's last speech, "What shadows have offended," and then thinking of these fairies as shadows. So again we were in this palette of shadows: black, white, gray, sepia; this shadowed place. I think color affects our mood; it's beautiful or it's exciting; it does visceral things.

Working as part of a team

I think costumes have an enormous effect on the performer and on the whole stage picture. And that's important. I think that an actor can invent something amazing by herself, by himself, or in a group of actors on the stage, with no production support per se. But when they do have production support, we can make what they do so much richer. We give actors a context with which to work, and they become part of the whole dialogue about doing a production. But if what we do doesn't release who they are, or who their characters are, we aren't listening.

If I were to design *Waiting for Godot*, I would talk to the two actors playing those parts, and I think that's a piece in which you have to work really closely with those two men. You have to have a vision of what that world is, and that will come from where it was written, where we are now, and what the language feels like now. But on the deepest level it's going to come through dialogue with those actors. Or with the director. It would start with the director, but I would hope that the four of us would sit down and talk about that world with the other designers.

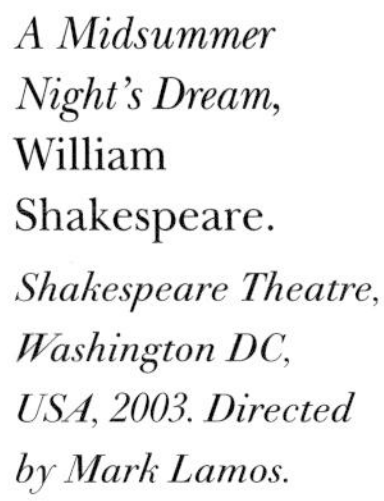

A Midsummer Night's Dream, William Shakespeare.
Shakespeare Theatre, Washington DC, USA, 2003. Directed by Mark Lamos.

080

A Midsummer Night's Dream, William Shakespeare. *Shakespeare Theatre, Washington DC, USA, 2003. Directed by Mark Lamos. Drawings for costume designs. Bottom right is Hippolyta as a bride. At the end of the play, all of the lovers were in white to emphasize the idea of them being interchangeable.*

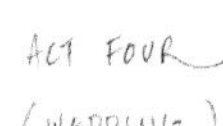

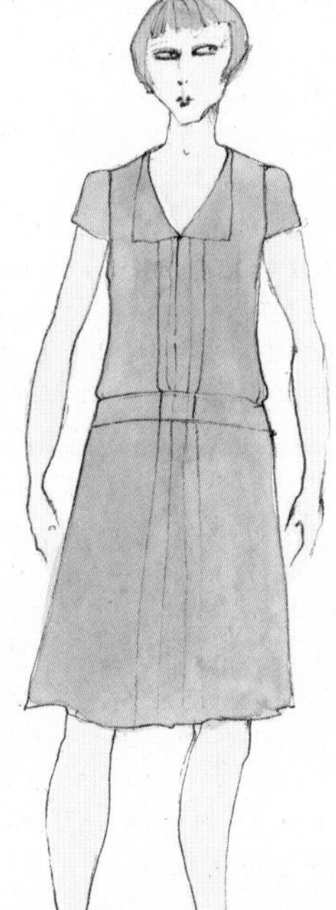

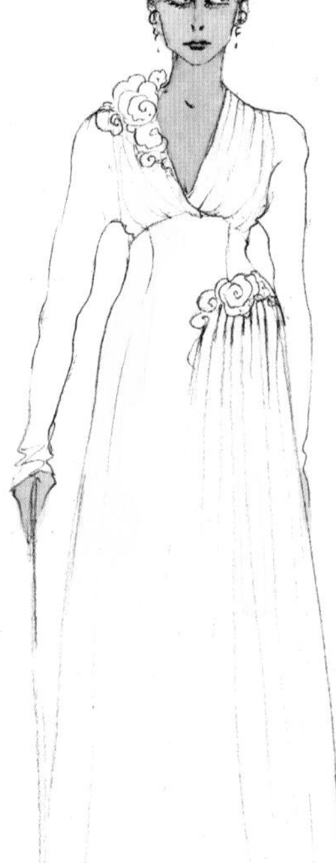

On costuming Shakespeare's Richards

We're rarely given the opportunity to have an early meeting with the actors, because they're not cast yet, or they're not paid yet, or they're just not around. But when I'm doing something like *Richard III*, I don't just hand Richard III his sketches and say, "This is what it's going to be." I sit down and we talk: about the character and about what kind of psychic approach that actor feels—what he's been thinking about that character—because that's such an important starting point. And what is his power, what are his vulnerabilities, what are his weaknesses, and how does he compensate for them? If you read the *Henry VI* plays, Richard is a younger man, a boy, in those plays—in the middle of the Wars of the Roses, surrounded by all his hotshot brothers, trying to get their attention, perhaps. So it's interesting to look through all the history plays and see what Richard's life story has been, as written by Shakespeare.

I've done *Henry VI*, the trilogy, twice; and I've done *Richard III* twice, as well as *Richard II*. So I've spent several years living those plays. And Richard's a fascinating character.

I design for the character. All different designs for the different Richards—basically I've designed four Richards. They were all extremely different. The first one was the most naïve, in a way. It was very early in my career as well. What I learned on that production was that the longer he rehearsed (this is Richard Thomas playing the part), the less he needed the hump and all the stuff that we were talking about designing. We gradually reduced those elements until he really didn't have many bells and whistles; it was just his physicality that created different things within the text. So I find that the better an actor you have in that part, the less stuff you need. But you have to go into it completely open to whatever that actor may involve. There's no point in imposing a design on someone playing Richard. You just have to be right by his side, working together.

The secret of excellent design

For me, a production design is excellent if it succeeds on all levels: if it's appropriate to surprise and delight me, and it does; but if it's costumed as a simple sweater and a slip, and it breaks my heart, that's also what I want. And if it works in a large sense: that it works logically in the story, in the world this production is bringing to the stage (whatever that interpretation is); that it's credible within the context of the approach to the whole production; and, most importantly, that it's absolutely right for the character, that the character is strengthened and illuminated by what they're wearing; that you immediately get it, and understand why they made that choice. And, as I said before, whether that involves the simplest thing or some kind of spectacular thing doesn't really matter to me. The aesthetics of it are beside the point. Whether it's beautiful or not is determined for me by whether or not it's right. "Right" meaning right for that character, which means in your gut. But also credible in the world that is being created.

That sense of design that comes from the gut—it comes from having an instinct and knowing how to follow it through, knowing how to give it life, give it shape, and stick to it as you design. Saying, "Now I'm clear on what this needs to be." I'll do a drawing, I'll put it on the page, but it has to remain the right choice—and be changed to remain your choice or become a better choice throughout the process of the production, with the performer, with the director. It's not just about saying, "This is the drawing, and this is what it's going to do." Sometimes it is right for everybody and you don't need to adjust it, except for the way it fits. But sometimes it doesn't feel right. If you have an actor who's a totally different kind of person and is never going to be the thing that you drew, then immediately you have to reassess and change it.

"Costume design has to be a combination of inspiration and intellect and technical information."

I feel that if you get your head straight about what something is, then your gut response can be free, you don't have to struggle with it. If you have that kind of intellectual discipline, then you can be playful. And for me it's a balancing act between those two things. Whether it's a drawing that's coming from my gut or from my head—first, it's coming from inside me. And I think that in drawing you have to become the character for a while in order to discover what their physicality is, and what the design is. Even if you're doing a completely straight-from-the-book 19th-century uniform, you have to draw the character who's wearing it, the way that it's worn, what it is about his uniform that looks like that person's uniform and not something out of a box—and that comes from the gut. But you're also using what you know about how the clothes need to be, where the seams are.

What costume designers do simultaneously is create. Not all drawings will or can do this, but you're creating a kind of blueprint for the people who make the clothes to look at and say, "I know what that is, I can make that. That's where you want that seam, that's what the proportion is." At the same time, you're doing all this work about how you feel about it, what the character feels like, and how you feel about the piece. So it has to be a combination of inspiration and intellect and technical information. The set designer has a set of blueprints in addition to the sketches, and I guess that's what research is in the context of costume. Research in many ways serves the purpose of blueprints, because you show them a photograph of a uniform and you say, "This is what the uniform is." But then you have to go back to your drawing and say, "This is how I changed it, and this is what I really want." And maybe your drawing is too suggestive and free for the character and your feeling at that moment, so then you have to do another drawing. And then you work in collaboration with the technicians who make the clothes and you sort it all out.

Opera versus theater

I don't really have a preference between opera and theater. I like doing good work, a good piece, good material with good directors. At the moment I'm doing a lot of opera, but last year I didn't do so much. Last year one of the most time-consuming projects I was involved in was Bette Midler's music tour. I do a bit of everything, I guess. I have found that I have a particular connection to music, to theater with music.

Broadway would be okay, but I'm not often drawn to your typical Broadway musical. I don't go to a lot of them. I loved *Urine Town,* I thought that was a fantastic piece. I liked its style, because it was conscious of what it was.

On theatrical inspirations

I guess the most influential theater designer would be Pina Bausch. [Pina Bausch founded the European Dance Theater genre.] She blows my mind. I love watching what she does. She completely amazes me ... The first piece I saw of hers was *Palermo, Palermo.* From the cinder block wall falling down, it just completely blew me away.

I think her design sense, her aesthetics, are impeccable. And they are mainly just old clothes. And they're beautiful old clothes. It's astonishing that they even stay together. And there's a humanness to them, and how they're used and what they mean. They're not just clothes—they become other things, they're transformational.

I was out of town while her piece was at BAM [Brooklyn Academy of Music] this year, and the people that I talked to who had seen it said, "Oh, it's not the best one we've seen." But somebody said, "It's like you have a good friend, and love going to dinner parties at that friend's house, and not every dinner party is equally good, but you really love going." And I thought that was a fair way of looking at her work. Sometimes it's less satisfying, but sometimes it seems like it's just meant to be.

There was one piece set in a big dark room, with a big dark wall, a big dark-paneled construct. And it seemed to be all about frustrated expectation and delayed gratification. But I thought that was the point—at least it was to me. Just to capture what you're after. In a way it's harder when you're working with a group and you're all trying to reach that kind of organic, seamless world where everything comes together and feels natural to itself. Anyway, I admire Bausch very much.

Biography

Constance Hoffman has designed costumes for opera, dance, and theater regionally, internationally, and in New York City. Her credits include collaborations with theater artists such as Mark Lamos, Julie Taymor, Eliot Feld, and Mikhail Baryshnikov; opera directors David Alden, Christopher Alden, and Keith Warner; and entertainer Bette Midler. On her Broadway debut, she earned a Tony nomination and an Outer Critics Circle Award for her designs for *The Green Bird*, directed by Julie Taymor. Her collaborations in opera have taken her to the Tel Aviv Opera, Bayerische Staatsoper in Munich, Oper Frankfurt, and Tokyo. In the United States she has designed costumes for the New York City Opera, San Francisco Opera, Houston Grand Opera, Los Angeles Opera, Minnesota Opera, Portland Opera, Opera Theatre of St. Louis, Florida Grand Opera, Virginia Opera, and has had a long association with the Glimmerglass Opera in Cooperstown, New York. Regionally she has designed in theaters such as the Guthrie, the Hartford Stage, the Shakespeare Theatre in Washington, DC, The Center Stage in Baltimore, The Alley Theatre in Houston, Goodspeed Musicals, and the Prince Music Theater. Hoffman was honored in 2001 with the Theatre Development Fund's Irene Sharaff Young Masters Award, and in 2003 with an invitation to exhibit her work in the Prague Quadrennial. From 2000 to 2004 she taught costume design at New York University's Tisch School of the Arts, and is now an adjunct professor there.

Ming Cho Lee

Set Design

Prominent set designer, Donald Oenslager professor, and co-chair of the design department at Yale School of Drama, Ming Cho Lee reflects on the radical transformation in his design approach since the 1960s. If in his previous approach he was emblematic, imposing an artistic idea on the design, in his current one he would prefer to let the design emerge from a close reading of the play. For Lee understanding, connecting, and living the life of the story fully is the starting point for design.

Mourning Becomes Electra, Eugene O'Neil.

The Shakespeare Theatre, Washington DC, USA, 1997. Directed by Michael Kahn.

Introduction

"I think my starting point today is very different from when I first started in the Sixties," observes Ming Cho Lee. The transformation was the result of a collaboration with director Liviu Ciulei on a production of *Hamlet*, where the two set out to explore and uncover all the details of the play in order to understand it completely. The result was a fully informed production, where the design and directing complemented each other and went hand in hand. Since then, Lee tries to get to the play "from the inside, rather than impose an outside idea on the design." He points out that "I have begun to appreciate and think more as a director." In this interview he describes the collaboration in detail, and then proceeds to give another example, using *Othello*.

In addition to insights into his design process, being co-chair of the Design department at Yale, Lee offers a full account of how he teaches, what he teaches, and what the strengths and weaknesses of some of the current students of design are.

La Boheme,
Giacomo Puccini.
American Opera Center, Juilliard School, New York, USA, 1972. Directed by Michael Cacoyanis. Model, 1/2in-scale for Acts I and IV. This design follows a very crude sketch idea from Cocoyanis. The sketch was made on yellow legal-pad paper. Lee believes that sketches should not become precious, hence used the cheapest paper possible.

La Boheme,
Giacomo Puccini.
American Opera Center, Juilliard School, New York, USA, 1972. Directed by Michael Cacoyanis. This production was not a high-concept production. It was performed in period and with no change of locale.

"I try to get to the play from the inside, rather than impose an outside idea on the design."

Approach

I think my starting point today is very different from when I first started in the Sixties. Then, I was more interested in the visual aspects, the visual character, and the visual statement about the work, and I tended to want to force the director to think as a designer. Today I seldom start strictly from a visual point of view. I try to get to the play from the inside, rather than impose an outside idea on the design. I have begun to appreciate and think more as a director.

The person who affected me most directly was Liviu Ciulei, when we did *Hamlet* together at Arena Stage. Liviu had just come to the States and felt that simply to direct was hard enough; he didn't want to take on the responsibility of designing. Of course I was very honored, so we met and I said, "Liviu, you're a designer, how would you want to approach this production?" And he said, "*Hamlet* is a mirror to nature. I think perhaps we should have mirrors." Today I would say that is a generalized statement, which you could apply to any play. So why *Hamlet*?

I was terribly uneasy about that approach, so I said, "It has a danger of becoming bad design. Let me ask you a question: when do you want to set your *Hamlet*?" A *Hamlet* happening in the 1400s or earlier would be a very different *Hamlet* from one that happened in the Renaissance—because in 1400 you'd still be trying to get away from overwhelming Catholicism, whereas in the Renaissance a secular aspect informed the world. Liviu said, "Well, if I can make the language work, if it doesn't feel jarring, I would like to do *Hamlet* at the turn of the century: 1890, 1900, 1905, 1910 ... pre-World War I, because at that time our grandparents, our parents were alive, and I know who these people were and how they behaved." Also at that time there were several publications—what Liviu called "Family Albums of Kings and Queens." He said, "They are wonderful books, I'll send them to you, and then we should start from there." But he still said, "I have to make sure the language works."

I thought that was a great idea, because in the abstract sense that period was about the death of monarchy, and certainly on one level *Hamlet* is about the end of the Danish monarchy. So I began to look at the books, at the people, to see what they would look like and how they would behave. I saw a picture of the British prime minister, Anthony Eden, who succeeded Churchill. Eden was a very handsome man, but was incompetent as a prime minister. We had talked a bit about Polonius. He is a very important person: he is literally taking care of the state, except that he has gotten senile and doesn't realize it—so it occurred to me that perhaps Polonius should have the look of Anthony Eden.

Mourning Becomes Electra, Eugene O'Neil.
The Shakespeare Theatre, Washington DC, USA, 1997. Directed by Michael Kahn.

Mourning Becomes Electra, Eugene O'Neil.
The Shakespeare Theatre, Washington DC, USA, 1997. Directed by Michael Kahn.

Set design through knowledge of people

I was the set designer, but I'm talking about people's faces, the way they carry themselves and what they wear, and how they behave, because if I know the people, the world is very easy to create. If I don't know the people, then it is a struggle. You're trying to create something that has no connection, no context. But what happened is that Liviu brought his books, and we went through them and looked at some of the big figures. We'd say, "That woman looks like Gertrude." Then there would be a German general and we'd say, "I think that is the ghost." So we'd go through the books and not talk about set design at all. Strictly about the play, the people: how they carry themselves, what they wear, how they eat and drink.

For me, it was like a world opening up. I have never done a Shakespeare with such a sense of immediacy and knowledge of the people. I had done *Hamlet* in numerous ways, and many of them tended to be very emblematic and formalistic. This time, because of Liviu, we went totally another way.

One problem was that Liviu and I knew exactly what the people looked like, but we did not include the costume designer! So we were speaking a language the costume designer had no inkling of, but eventually she got caught up. Then, even before we really designed the set, I said, "How would you do the ghost?" And Liviu said, "Well, the fact that we're doing it at the turn of the century, when the ghost comes out—I think there should be organ music." So we actually talked about music and sound. I said, "How would you do the play within the play?" And Liviu said, "I think this is an acting troupe that is actually a little down-and-out, with older actors wearing over-coats. If possible, I think the music should be a string quartet" (although we didn't use that).

Then I approached the set. I started by taking the existing stage floor out. By then it was the second time it had been done at Arena Stage. It created a pit, and I thought, "We'll float a platform in the middle, with staircases going down into the basement." I looked at pictures of St. Martin on the Strand in London. The parquet floor of the church is beautifully finished—kind of black. I said, "Here is this beautifully finished floor, and below is a labyrinth of brick vaulting." Then I thought, "Why not line the sides of the pit with mirror? Then people will see the reflection of the brick vaulting underneath this very finished floor." I made a little model and Liviu loved it, although he was nervous about material that is fake. He thought that wood would be better, because it would have been constructed from real materials. By then I'd learned not to be so protective about my ideas, and if someone gave me a suggestion, I'd try it. I tried the wood and said,

"Liviu, it's beginning to look like *Billy Budd*." And he said, "You're right, we'll do brick, white brick." Then we included the mirror, lining the pit, and it was fascinating. You'd sit in the audience and look at the stage, and see the mirror wall of the pit, showing the brick support vaulting, underneath the platform. It was a real labyrinth. You never knew where it began and ended. And that was the set. We had the trapdoor open and the ghost came up from below. Occasionally there was an opening in the platform, so that people could see through the trap and see the labyrinth underneath. The more abstract idea was that everything seems perfect on the surface, but that underneath it's all rotten. And all that came directly out of our conversation about people. The behavior of the people is controlled and socially correct on the surface, but has so many undercurrents that the contrast between the parquet floor on top and the complex brick vaulting underneath seemed right.

The design was approved and we were building it. Liviu called and said, "I have a crazy idea." The Ophelia mad scene, if you're not careful, always sounds operatic—like Lucia's mad scene. "What if," he said, "Claudius and Gertrude are giving a welcome-home dinner party for the ambassador he sent to Norway, and Ophelia is included?" Which means that we should have the table set with the best tablecloth, silk with trim; the best silverware and crystal; and, as the centerpiece, bowls of dried flowers and so forth … And Ophelia is wearing black, because she is in mourning for Polonius. After saying grace, they all sit down and start to eat, and Ophelia tears off her black dress and starts singing bawdy songs. I have to tell you, that is the best Ophelia mad scene I have ever experienced.

Then, just before we started rehearsal, Liviu said that after reading the play again, he realized that before the final scene—the duel—nobody but Laertes and Claudius knew that there would be bloodshed. We've become so familiar with the story: we know that everyone dies; but in the play nobody knows, except Laertes and Claudius. So Liviu said, "I think it should look like a tennis match." And so, both of us agreed, they should all wear white. And again, because we are in the time period where we know what things look like, we said we should have green runners and white wicker furniture. And we knew exactly what kind of decanter the wine should be in, what kind of glass, and so forth. Everyone wore white and … total bloodshed.

It was an experience I'll never forget, and I realized that, when you try to envisage the world for a play, instead of thinking architecturally, you may want to think about the people; you may want to think about the music; you may want to think about what they drink; what are they doing. And ever

La Boheme,
Giacomo Puccini.
American Opera Center, Juilliard School, New York, USA, 1972. Directed by Michael Cacoyanis. Sketch for Act II. The sketch was done in a hotel room following a visit to various covered arcades in Paris. "The best kind of research is on-site research."

La Boheme,
Giacomo Puccini.
American Opera Center, Juilliard School, New York, USA, 1972. Directed by Michael Cacoyanis. This 1/2in-scale model does not include the necessary furniture.

"When you try to envisage the world for a play, instead of thinking architecturally, you may want to think about the people; you may want to think about the music; you may want to think about what they drink; what are they doing."

King John, William Shakespeare.
The Shakespeare Theatre, Washington DC, USA, 1999. Directed by Michael Kahn.

Peer Gynt, Henrik Ibsen.
The Shakespeare Theatre, Washington DC, USA, 1998. Directed by Michael Kahn. Model, 1/2-in scale.

since then I tend to read plays more carefully. Whenever I have a problem, I'll simply read the play and see what's going on: what is the action, what are they doing? Very often I will say, "Now, what happened in that opening scene?" What are they doing? Are they standing or sitting? If someone's sitting, there should be a chair. The way I approach designing now is very different. Perhaps because I'm getting old, I'm becoming much more flexible, less judgmental. I no longer feel that doing realism is a crime. I've discovered that doing realism is the hardest thing you can do—everything has to be so real, how do you do it? You can't have anything that's fake. I've also begun to trust my instincts a bit more. If I read the play and see that, above all, things should have an emotional quality much more than an architectural quality, I'll go for it. So at this point, interestingly enough, I find designing much more enjoyable and feel less pressured.

Working with directors

I actually love working with directors now. In the early days I did not, because I was always trying to force them to speak my language. Now I speak their language and I can talk about a play and get excited with them. I can talk about what's going on and ask cogent questions, so directors enjoy working with me and I enjoy working with them. I love working with Jon Jory, for example. I did a lot of Shakespeare with him at the Actors Theatre of Louisville. For the *Othello* we did, we agreed that the two women walk into a totally man-centered military world. There are no other women there. They are all men who are geared to fight. Jon said he had been in the army, and that the army mentality was horrible—frightening, explosive, and filled with macho-ness. And here are two women. If Othello had been in Venice, he would have had friends and someone would have said, "What are you doing, listening to that Iago?" But in Cyprus the first thing Iago did was to get rid of Cassio. So the only person Othello could talk to was Iago—and that is death. The idea that you can actually explore a real spirit of evil is amazing. So we talked about it, and we said that it seems much better to do *Othello* in the 1960s—instead of in the Renaissance, where everything is remote and picturesque and a costume drama. I have always wanted to do a contemporary *Othello*, where all the embassies or consulates are totally soulless compounds. So I said I would love to design a set that looked like a Holiday Inn! I have to say, it is one of the most powerful *Othellos* I have ever experienced. I've done a lot of *Othellos*, but this one stood out.

This was a collaboration between director and designer, because we talked about what we thought would make the play really live today. Jon wanted to do it in a military setting because he was close to the experience, and I have always said that *Othello* happens in a military community in a foreign land. For me, that is a way of getting inside the play and letting the play inform you. If you're trying to get that kind of idea by thinking about architecture or metaphor, you will never get there. But the fact that it's a personal experience—that I've been to Moscow, to the American Embassy and the ambassador's house, and it's horrible—I felt that would be the right place, a kind of a building that had no soul. And there, you have two women; the third woman in the camp is a prostitute. So the two of them, Emilia and Desdemona, have absolutely no chance. They don't even have another woman to talk to.

For me, at this point, my instinct in reading the play is important. When I start reading, I try not to analyze too carefully. I try to imagine myself seeing the play for the first time. Of course I can't help but think visually, but the most important thing is: does the play have an impact on me? Am I moved? Is it funny? So for me the first reading of the play has to be that sort of instinctive connection. If you don't connect with the play, you'll have a hard time doing it. If it connects, then with the second and third reading you have something to start from. You can look for pictures and you have images in your head, so that when you talk to a director, you're a designer and not a blank page. But at the same time you haven't formulated any real approach.

Then I start asking questions to see if the director is connecting to the play in the same way. What time do you want it set in, and why? If you want to set it in the Renaissance, how do you prevent this production from becoming a costume drama? And perhaps, in order to do it in the Renaissance, we may have to talk about it in contemporary terms, in order to find out how those people relate to us, and then take it back to the Renaissance. I never design costumes, but interestingly, today I would not start working on a show without a costume designer. At least, if we don't have a costume designer, I would have thought through—much like *Hamlet*—how people would look, so that I can enter the world that gives those people context.

I think that between the director and designer there is no need for a meeting to talk strictly about design. I think the director should tell the designer what he or she tells the actors. And as a designer, if you have a very strong view about the design—the world of the play—you should say so. When they're uncertain, directors use a lot of catch phrases like, "I don't want to be realistic." But maybe it's a very realistic play! What does that mean? What are you going to tell the actors? Don't act realistically? I also hear directors say, "I do very physical theater." What does that mean? Sometimes a lack of physical action is very physical. For me, a designer has a lot more to grab onto if the director shares with them what he or she plans to tell the actors. And you should certainly talk about how you feel about a play.

The reason that designers are so important to directors is that, in American theater, three-quarters of the choices have already been made before an actor even says one word. That's why directors are so nervous about committing. On the other hand, the designers have to be the best dramaturgs, in order to work with a director rather than forcing the director into some visual theory.

Working with other design elements

Costume, for me, is actually the starting point. I get to know the people, and get a sense of when it happened, and sometimes I do research about the people. So their clothes have a reality. As for light, I used to do lighting, so I always have a sixth sense about it. When I design a set I am always very conscious of how the lighting should be. Sound, I think, is much like costumes. For example, on *Twelfth Night* at Stratford, Connecticut, I asked Jerry Freedman what kind of music, and he said James Morris was writing it. Immediately there was no conversation. I didn't have a reference; I didn't have anything that related to the people in the play.

When I'm designing, sometimes costume may be there—a little drawing of figures—but when you start adding in lights, you can cheat too much; it becomes about the physical production, rather than concentrating on the actors and what they are doing. So sometimes when I find myself unable to go further, I'll do a storyboard and then, as the storyboard gets clearer, I may add lighting. But usually at the beginning it's very crude; it's usually line drawings. I'm careful not to let atmosphere get in the way.

I'm a person who keeps trying to find out the facts. I tell my students I don't think you can draw adjectives. "Oh, it's 'beautiful'"—what do you draw? Or they'll say "It's magic"—how do you draw "magic?" Or they'll say, "It's theatrical"—well, I don't know what "theatrical" means! But if you ask, during that scene, what are Othello and Iago doing? Are they just standing up there talking to each other, or are they doing business? Iago may be opening a briefcase with documents, and while he is giving Othello the documents he says, "That Cassio over there—what is he doing there?" "Oh, don't worry about it." Now everything has a context. So I keep asking, "What are the facts?" You can draw facts. You can draw people talking to each other doing things, but I don't know how you draw "magic." When people say the designer isn't imaginative enough, I don't know what that means! Imagination comes out of being able to grab the facts and let them fly, bringing them into reality.

On good design

If there are a lot of abstractions and so forth, then I don't know where the characters are or where the play takes place. But if I see someone who does a design for *Trojan Women*, and it's set in a place that I'd never thought of, and it brings *Trojan Women* a sense of grounded reality, then I no longer need all the Greek tragedy formality and so forth.

For example, there was one person, an NYU student, who set *Trojan Women* in an abandoned hotel ballroom or lobby. I thought it was a wonderful idea, but she didn't go far enough. I said, "Troy is destroyed—this hotel ballroom is a mess. The women are imprisoned there, so not only is the ballroom filled with beds, but perhaps the window is all covered with plywood; there's rubble all over, wire hanging down." That, for me, is a design that has a point of view. That designer has a director's point of view. You know pretty much exactly how those people will behave and why.

Annie, Strouse, Charnin, and Meehan.

A touring production for the thirtieth Anniversary of Annie, *USA, 2005. Directed by Martin Charnin. Model, 1/4in-scale, for the orphanage.*

Annie, Strouse, Charnin, and Meehan.

A touring production for the thirtieth Anniversary of Annie, *USA, 2005. Directed by Martin Charnin. Model, 1/4in-scale, for the east room.*

"Theater that is all about messages is boring theater. I hate earnest theater with a message."

If there is something visually very exciting, I would certainly acknowledge that. Last year, for example, there was a student from Long Beach whom I invited to the Clambake. [Believing in the importance of nurturing and mentoring future theater artists of America, Lee founded the design portfolio review known as "Ming's Clambake," which brings graduating students from major theater design programs together with professional designers and directors in a weekend-long review of their work.] He had done a model for *King Lear* that was set on an oil rig. It was very exciting to look at, as a piece of sculpture for an installation. "How are you going to do *King Lear* there?" I asked him. "Is the first scene just on the oil rig? There is no luxury there. What does Lear have to lose?" Now *King Lear* is about many things, but if you want to talk about it, you will eventually face a time when there is nothing. Nothing.

I've always said that without Shakespeare's *King Lear* there could be no Samuel Beckett ... At the depth of *King Lear*, when two old men are running around in this wilderness talking nonsense to each other, now that is Samuel Beckett. But when they have nothing—where did they come from? Where were they? What were they wearing? How did they act, when they had a lot of wealth? So *King Lear* is about a "before" and an "after," and if you only have after and no before, then how can you do it?

This is why I ask these questions; not to tell students how to do it, but to encourage them to think. For example, if the students are doing a play they have selected and they have very highfalutin, abstract ideas for it, such as "The world is a stage" or "Everyone is an actor," or if someone said, "Oh, Hedda Gabler is trapped, so we'll design a set that is a trap," then I'll respond by saying, "Name me a play where the leading character is not trapped. Why is this specifically for *Hedda Gabler* and not for *A Doll's House*?" This is the way I teach, now. I ask these questions. "Why is this specifically for this play?"

Teaching design

I teach design by critique. There are very few lectures. When they come in, I might say, "This comes from nowhere. Have you done storyboards? Perhaps you should do a storyboard." Michael Yeargan and I always look at the students' designs and see what is needed, or what makes no sense, and then zero in on that and ask a lot of questions: "Why have you chosen to do that?" "How do you read the play?" Very often we'll say, "You know, I don't think you like the play." And the students will answer, "No, really ... I find it really boring" or "I hate the characters." "Well, why do you hate the characters?" "Because they are all so nasty." "Well, that's what the play is all about!" If someone says, "I hate *Othello* because Iago is so evil, and I hate evil characters," then don't do the play! Can you imagine a play without conflict? Then what is theater? Can you imagine a world without conflict, or life without conflict? Theater that is all about messages is boring theater. I hate earnest theater with a message. So this is how I teach.

We assign projects and now I insist that they come in with a portrait gallery—only photographs. Paintings would be useless 99 percent of the time. And sometimes they have wonderful portrait galleries, and out of that they sometimes design a very abstract set, and I ask, "Can you imagine these people living in your world?" And for all of them, except designers, I don't ask for drawings, unless they feel they want to do them. They just come in with portrait galleries and research, and for a project of two weeks that's almost enough. I'm tailoring my design class to playwrights, directors, and designers, and forcing the designers to think with the directors.

I have sound designers as well, so whenever something is off, I ask, "What is the music?" For sound designers I would ask them, "In *The Seagull*, what is Constantine playing two rooms away? Whose music is he playing? Schubert? Tchaikovsky? Schumann? Who?"

I would not design costume myself. First of all, I don't do it as well, but also I love having an exciting costume designer—especially at the beginning when we are exploring, "Let's do it in this period, or multiple periods," or whatever. As for lighting, I would never do lighting, but I understand it. I think of lighting a great deal. But I don't illustrate it.

I would say the best collaboration is when you have a leader, usually in the person of the director, who has an overall vision—an approach that he or she would like the play to have. If it's exciting enough, all the designers and actors somehow go for the same vision; and if it falls apart, it falls apart. Nothing is guaranteed. Someone probably is not with it. Vision is a point of view. There is a personal commitment to it. It comes from one person, a leader's connection with the work, and why it is important to the work. It's good enough to say, "I want with this scene not to have a dry eye in the house." Or "At the end of *Hamlet,* when everyone dies, I don't want anyone to breathe, because it is so horrifying."

I now feel that sometimes doing a great rough sketch may be the best starting point. I don't do renderings at all and I discourage people from doing them. The European designers don't do renderings. But I encourage doing storyboards, rough sketches, always tied in with a ground plan that will help you get started making a 1/8-inch model. At Yale, costume designers and sound designers take set design too, and set designers take costume design. And for electives, we encourage designers to take a directing class.

The challenges of teaching

I changed my style and I changed my way of teaching, and I'm constantly questioning my own design. So, at least right now, occasionally my students feel that I'm forcing them into something. And I do, very often I do. Because if someone's doing a production and they're not getting there, finally I say, "Okay, would you just try this? Because if you don't, I have no idea whether or not my suggestion would be good, and you're still not getting anywhere." Somewhere along the line the process was broken. And occasionally when I'm teaching directors I say, "You're not saying anything that a designer can pick up a pencil and draw."

Very often when you make a commitment, you can actually free yourself and explore many different things. If you want to have your cake and eat it too, then you get stuck. People say, "I don't want a costume drama or museum piece, but I don't want it set today either. I really just want no period." Usually my question is: how can a show have no period? Have you ever seen a show with no period? What does that mean? Usually it means many periods. That's all right with me, but how do you arrive at many periods? Your starting point is not many periods; it is exploring the show today, or putting it in the 1900s or the 1700s. Then you can deconstruct your world; but you can't deconstruct something until you have constructed something. So much of teaching is about process.

I find the difficult part of teaching design is when I have a student who came from graphics or fine arts and is getting into theater—thinking that theater is a magic box where they can do anything—but is not really interested in theater. They are not moved by seeing a show, they want to reduce everything to a metaphor. And I find that very difficult.

We have a lot of Korean and Japanese students (mostly women) and are now very careful when they come with little English. I'll say, "Go immerse yourself in English. Because even though you think you can be a designer because it's all visual, and you can draw, and so forth, you can't tell a story in the language"; or "When you read a play, you cannot connect with it because of language problems, so the process cannot begin." I have found that to be very, very difficult.

Annie, Strouse, Charnin, and Meehan.
A touring production for the thirtieth Anniversary of Annie, *USA, 2005. Directed by Martin Charnin. Model, 1/4in-scale, for Hooverville (59th Street bridge).*

Annie, Strouse, Charnin, and Meehan.
A touring production for the thirtieth Anniversary of Annie, *USA, 2005. Directed by Martin Charnin. Model, 1/4in-scale, for New York City (Times Square).*

King Lear, William Shakespeare.
Vivian Beaumont Theater, Lincoln Center, New York, USA, 1968. Directed by Gerald Freedman. Part of a 1/4in-scale storyboard showing the storm.

King Lear, William Shakespeare.
Vivian Beaumont Theater, Lincoln Center, New York, USA, 1968. Directed by Gerald Freedman. Model, 1/2in-scale.

"I think that sense of Brechtian reality—the emphasis on facts—will always stay with me."

I also find difficult people who want to reduce everything to visual terms and are not interested in telling the story. Imagine that you were growing up and no one told you any stories! How do you get to know your grandparents? So my thinking today—and I would say the turning point was working with Liviu—is quite different from when I started, perhaps because when I first started I had substantial language problems. I was always skirting the play trying to reduce it to visual terms, designing an emblematic set. Fortunately, what I was doing then was mostly Shakespeare. It always worked, because in Shakespeare you don't want to illustrate each scene, but rather give a sense of the whole, and I was very good at that. I look at those designs and see how in some way they changed the look of American scenic design, but today I find them a little bit cold and calculating. There's a lack of specifics and there's no emotional connection, which I feel I need now. That doesn't mean the design today is better than the earlier ones, but I have changed and I don't feel I can return to the earlier way.

On Brecht

Brecht is all facts, facts, facts, facts, facts! This is something I am still pushing. And because he wants you to search for facts, facts, facts, there is no emotional indulgence. But when you add it together, the greatest work is absolutely devastating. *Galileo* is devastating. What happened to the daughter? But I would say that was all before I was completely overwhelmed by this person called William Shakespeare. You know, without any Shakespeare there wouldn't be any Brecht. I've also found that it was very important that his approach to theater was very tough, very clear-headed, and not about fakery or illusions. The stage is not something else, or an illusion of something else. It is a stage and a finite space, not an attempt to recreate endless space. If you want an endless space in a finite space, how do you do it? Brook's empty space is the hardest thing to do. I've also found that the unsentimental approach to looking at the world is important, so that it doesn't become acting emotions. That usually makes for terrible theater. If you play what's happening, the emotion will come out of it.

I think Brecht will never leave me, although I no longer feel that I have to be only Brechtian. I think that sense of Brechtian reality—the emphasis on facts—will always stay with me. I would also have great problems doing a set that looked real, but was not real—if it was all an illusion. I have a problem with illusionistic theater or the illusion of space, unless it's really called for. Then there is always stagecraft and that can be very exciting, but maybe you want to make sure people know it's a stage trick. That's all my Brechtian side coming through.

On the qualities of a designer

So what are the basic ingredients in order to be a designer? I would say the designer must at least know how to draw—designing is transforming words into visual imagery. Any more words are a waste of time. When you meet up with the director, the words should already have been transformed into visual imagery. So that the director can react to it, your idea must be expressed through drawing. I don't understand how you could make a model without first doing some drawing. You can't just start cutting paper. Drawing is essential.

You must also know how to read, but that gets a little more complicated. I would say that if you have a language problem, then all bets are off. In US drama schools we teach Western theater, like it or not, so you have to be able to read the language and articulate your thoughts with clarity.

As the designer, you should be able to trust your instincts before you analyze too much. You then need to have a capacity to analyze. But, when you start analyzing as if you're writing a term paper, that's deadly. I'd say for a designer or a director, after you've read the play, can you tell the story in an exciting way? If you're telling the story to your friends and they fall asleep, you are not going to do a good job of directing. I think that's a starting point.

You have to love storytelling. You have to love sharing experience and being involved in the plays where experiences are shared. You experience a lot of things not because you live it, but because you live it through the theater, and that's as real as your real life.

But the foundation is that if you can't draw, you don't have a starting point. You can tell in prospective students' drawings of set designs whether they can draw at all. We always say, "If you have any other drawings—figure drawings or whatever—bring them." You can tell right away. They can show you a sketch, or a deadly rendering, and you know that person has a taste problem. That person cannot draw. That person's faking it. That person is using a computer to do all the work. It is very difficult to cheat in drawing.

On experimental, process-based theater I think that process is always trying something new. It's that, or copying something old and claiming it to be yours. If you have a point of view about the work you're doing, that doesn't mean that you don't look at other people's design. I had a student do terrific research for *Salome*, saying, "I think it takes place here," but then she went and did something else because she wouldn't copy her research. That's nonsense. If the research is great, plunk it on the stage and take a look. That's how you do research and that's how you use it. If you don't, then why do it? Recently, for example, I was doing *Christmas Carol*. This is industrial England of course. The design that informed me most was Ian MacNeil's design for *An Inspector Calls*. It's fantastic. It's a huge space, a London house on stilts—very much like Magritte—and covered with cobblestones, and raining all the time. I actually did Scrooge's house as a dead copy of MacNeil's design, but by the time I finished, it was no longer his design.

I doubt my own choices all the time. You say, "Great!" now, but two years later you say, "Garbage! I should have done something else." Or you say, "Today I would not do it that way." However, say today someone suggested, "Let's do an *Othello*," I would say, "I'm not ready, because of the fantastic experience I had with Jon Jory. At this point I don't have anything new to say."

For a long time I would have loved to do Verdi's operas. Now, of course, it's so difficult to do a Verdi opera because Verdi singers are no longer available. For a long time I wanted to do Verdi's *Othello*, but now, after seeing some *Othellos*—I think it is one of the greatest operas—I found it difficult to do, just because during the drinking scene you have 90 members of the chorus singing together. What kind of world do you create for that?

On Beckett versus Shakespeare

Waiting for Godot is very difficult. You know, Shakespeare tells many stories in one play. He is a master storyteller, until something like *Timon of Athens*, and even that is interesting. That actually became more Samuel Beckett than anything else. There are so many facets of life that he examined. With *Waiting for Godot* I've discovered that unless you find the real vaudeville music-hall comedy of it, it is a terribly boring play. I can't stand it unless it's funny! And it is very funny, but you have to discover that.

I designed one at the Washington Arena Stage, but I never sat through a dress rehearsal because I was usually in the lobby saying, "Oh my God …" It was a terrific design, but it was really boring. Then I did one with Brian Bedford in Stratford, Ontario, and I said, "Unless they play those tricks to the hilt, it is bloody boring." So we did it proceeding largely from an abandoned music hall with a dirty floor, and the idea of vaudeville. Then I discovered that what makes *Waiting for Godot* so difficult to design is that you shouldn't have any landmarks, because they never know where they are. Except for the tree. But the tree changes! "Gee, was this leaf here before? Where did it come from?" That's funny! Until you discover the humor, Samuel Beckett is hard to do. It's not hard to design, but it's hard to do: where do you grab hold of it?

Biography

Ming Cho Lee is one of the foremost set designers in America today, and is a recipient of the National Medal of Arts, the highest national award given in the arts. His extensive credits include work in opera, dance, and theater. He has worked with many leading American dance companies, including Martha Graham, the American Ballet Theatre, Joffrey Ballet, Eliot Feld Ballet, Jose Limon, and Pacific Northwest Ballet. From 1962 to 1973 he was the principal designer for Joseph Papp's New York Shakespeare Festival. He has designed sets for opera companies including the Metropolitan Opera, New York City Opera, Lyric Opera of Chicago, and San Francisco Opera. He has also designed for theater groups, including the Arena Stage, Mark Taper Forum, Guthrie Theater, Actors Theatre of Louisville, Seattle Repertory Theatre, and the Manhattan Theatre Club, as well as for Broadway. Internationally, Lee has designed productions for Covent Garden, London; Hamburgische Staatsoper; Teatro Colon, Buenos Aires; Royal Danish Ballet; Cloud Gate Dance Theatre, Taipei; the Hong Kong Cultural Centre; and Buhnen Graz, Austria. His numerous other awards and distinctions include a Tony Award, an Obie for sustained achievement, New York Drama Desk and New York and Los Angeles Outer Circle Critics Awards, three honorary doctorates, awards for long-term achievement from six major theater and opera organizations, membership in the Theater Hall of Fame, and the Mayor's Award for Arts and Culture from New York City. He holds the Donald Oenslager Chair in Design and is co-chair of the design department at the Yale University School of Drama.

Adrianne Lobel

Set Design

What makes Adrianne Lobel a unique designer is the fact that she can see and find the here and now in the plays and operas she designs. This is seen from as early on as her design work for *Marriage of Figaro* to her most recent works, such as *On the Town* and *Dr. Atomic*. For Lobel, process is synonymous with design, and she places a very high value on the design process and on what goes into the making of the final design.

On the Town,
Leonard Bernstein, Betty Comden, and Adolf Green.
Delacorte Theater, New York, USA, 1997. Directed by George Wolfe. Detail of process sketch.

Introduction

For Adrianne Lobel, the start of any production begins with listening to the music. "The music," she points out, "is the driving force for design." Once the music is on, she begins to sketch. Research is secondary—what comes out of her while she listens to the music will define what she wants to research at a later date.

The sense of the here and now permeates Lobel's work: it is there as she designs and it is there in the final set design. Talking about the process, she points out that what is important is keeping yourself amused and interested during the design process, because "If you're not very amused while you're working, no one's going to be amused looking at your work." In this sense, all her designs have a playfulness that shows she was having fun designing them. This is particularly true of her contemporary designs and contemporized pieces, which require a certain degree of playfulness in transposing the time period.

Dr. Atomic, John Adams and Peter Sellars.

San Francisco Opera, USA, 2005. Directed by Peter Sellars. Early model storyboard.

"The music is the driving force for the design. I can turn it off, but I have it so deeply ingrained in my body that it's still coming out my hand."

Approach

My starting point is the material itself, as it is for a director. If it's a music piece—and I find that I've been working more and more on music pieces—you need to know what the story is and then you want to listen to the music. And the music is the driving force for the design. In my case I will not start sketching until I have that music on. That music is moving my hand, in the beginning. Later on I can turn it off, but I have it so deeply ingrained in my body that it's still coming out my hand. So, that is primary. Research is secondary.

First, I want to have an instinctive reaction visually to the music. What comes out when I'm listening to the music will define what I'm going to research later. In other words, when I'm designing *Marriage of Figaro*, I don't rush out and look at 18th-century paintings of Fragonard. It's going to guide me in the wrong direction—in a direction that's not terribly interesting.

If you ask, "How do you get from A to B?" that's the key. Learning how to keep moving in the process—if you've hit a roadblock, how to move away from that roadblock and keep going—is the process of design. How not to get stuck, how to keep interested, how to amuse yourself, because if you're not very amused while you're working, no one's going to be amused looking at your work. You create an excitement for yourself and that will translate later into the design. It's the same thing as when a choreographer shows you what music looks like on dancers' bodies; a designer shows you what music looks like in the scenery. You're listening to the music and you're drawing while it goes. And you're drawing different parts of it, and if one part is inspiring in particular, you just keep repeating it over and over. In *Figaro* it's the overture, so I listened to the overture over and over again. You do what you need to do to juice yourself up. Keep up the excitement. The sketches that I did for *Dr. Atomic*, the new John Adams opera, were so much fun. It's like being a jazz musician. You're drawing jazz riffs. And it's as loose and childlike as you could possibly be, to get to the guts of the matter.

Working with directors

In the beginning you don't necessarily know which direction you want to go toward. Certainly you have an initial discussion with the director. The director fills you in on the history of a piece, and sometimes has a very strong take on the piece himself or herself. Most of the directors I've worked with do not say, "I want it to be that" or "I want it to be this." They do not have a concept fully developed, which I then have to follow. They usually leave it to me, because my process of discovery is going to be their process of discovery, and we go through it together. So I do very rough sketches in the beginning,

"Everyone brings their own influences to a production. Collaboration doesn't mean a weakening of someone's vision. Collaboration means many people's visions coming together."

Dr. Atomic, John Adams and Peter Sellars.

San Francisco Opera, USA, 2005. Directed by Peter Sellars. Set piece in the shop: the "gadget."

Dr. Atomic, John Adams and Peter Sellars.

San Francisco Opera, USA, 2005. Directed by Peter Sellars.

and I will then have a director come and see where things are leading so that they can have an input at various stages of the process.

It's a collaborative effort. Everyone brings their own influences to a production. Collaboration doesn't mean a weakening of someone's vision. Collaboration means many people's visions coming together. And a good director's job is being able to edit a number of artists in a room into a fantastic fabric. It doesn't mean that there's a dictatorship. It doesn't mean that a director will say, "This is it—this is my vision. You must do as I say." I wouldn't be interested in that. I'm interested in bringing my own artistic impulses, my own concepts, my own (sometimes very strong) ideas to a production. And I'm interested in working with other people who are going to do that same thing. When a concept—a visual concept for a show—is strong enough, it can hold all the other ideas. And that goes for a director's concept, too.

On the designs for *Marriage of Figaro*

When I worked with Peter Sellars on *Marriage of Figaro*, the idea of a penthouse came about directly from the drawings. I got ideas while I was drawing. I said to myself, "Maybe I should look at this. Maybe I should look at that." And then I went out and researched, and then I presented him with drawings of Trump Tower and he said, "This is it!" and then figured out how to really use it. But that concept was born visually.

To get from Mozart to Trump Tower, I listened to Mozart. A lot of very baroque shapes came through. They looked like French curve shapes and sort of like Frank Stella sculptures; there was a Frank Stella sculpture in the third act. So sometimes you go back to the very original impulse and you just make a sort of in-joke for yourself about it. The problem with *Figaro* is that you can't be all Lucy-goosey-Lucy about it. It's a very iron-clad plot, works like clockwork. The da Ponte libretto is like a Kaufman and Hart play. Machines that work! You gotta know where the rooms are; there has to be real architecture. So a lot of curly-swirly stuff is not really going to lead you anywhere.

When Peter and I first met, he said he wanted it to be about New York, but we didn't know where in New York. It could have been a townhouse on the Upper East Side; it could have been a prewar building on the Upper West Side. But, in thinking about the hierarchy of the piece—that there were chauffeurs and maids, and cooks and nannies, and what have you, which is all true of life in New York for very rich people. This is the Eighties we're talking about too, when Trump was at his all-time most powerful. There was this

On the Town, Leonard Bernstein, Betty Comden, and Adolf Green. *Delacorte Theater, New York, USA, 1997. Directed by George Wolfe. Early sketch.*

On the Town, Leonard Bernstein, Betty Comden, and Adolf Green. *Delacorte Theater, New York, USA, 1997. Directed by George Wolfe. Production photograph.*

asshole count, who thought that if he felt like sleeping with the maid, he could, because of who he was. And the aspect of Fragonard did come into it a little bit, because when I thought about 18th-century paintings by Watteau and Boucher and Fragonard, and the things you normally associate with Mozart productions, you think about those clouds—those puffy, pink, 18th-century clouds. Well, where do you see puffy, pink, 18th-century clouds in New York? Up high in the sky through glass.

And then the idea of high and low: the poor are down there, the high are up here and never even set foot on the ground. So the more I thought about these things, the more it led to—and it was also in the drawing—a glass tower, and then the glass tower led to a more specific idea, which was Trump Tower. And then I had it! And then you have to know that the door to the laundry room led to the count's bedroom, which is next to, you know ... You must have a sense of how the apartment is laid out.

Concerning *On the Town*

These sketches are for *On the Town*. I listened to the music, and it's Bernstein and it's New York and it's also the park. This was the original design for the Delacorte Theater in Central Park. It was a very exciting event. It worked less well on Broadway because the original impulse was for the park—a free event and an incredible Valentine to New York. But there's nothing out there; it's an empty flat floor with the hills and a turtle pond in the background. I wanted to make the most of the surround, but it's also a musical where you have to bring scenery on and off, so I knew I had to create some kind of structure that held tracks and that could bring things on and off. I had to create the theater machine to bring on the little pieces of scenery I was going to design. And I also wanted it to be very open and airy so that you could see through it. I knew that I wanted it to be sort of lacy and steely, and that it had to be practical. And I also had to figure out where to put the band. I knew there was a lot of dancing, so it had to have a big empty floor, too.

These are the problems that you have to start with. They're technical and creative. One thing is absolutely the other. So here I am, drawing to Bernstein. I don't know what I'm drawing; I'm drawing in the space. And I use tracing paper a lot. And sometimes I'll come in in the morning and look at all the sketches I did the day before, so that I can get into the groove. So here we have what looks a bit like Grand Central Station, and here's the skyline and there's a little apartment and there's people up here, because I felt from the start that the band had to be off the floor somehow and part of the machinery.

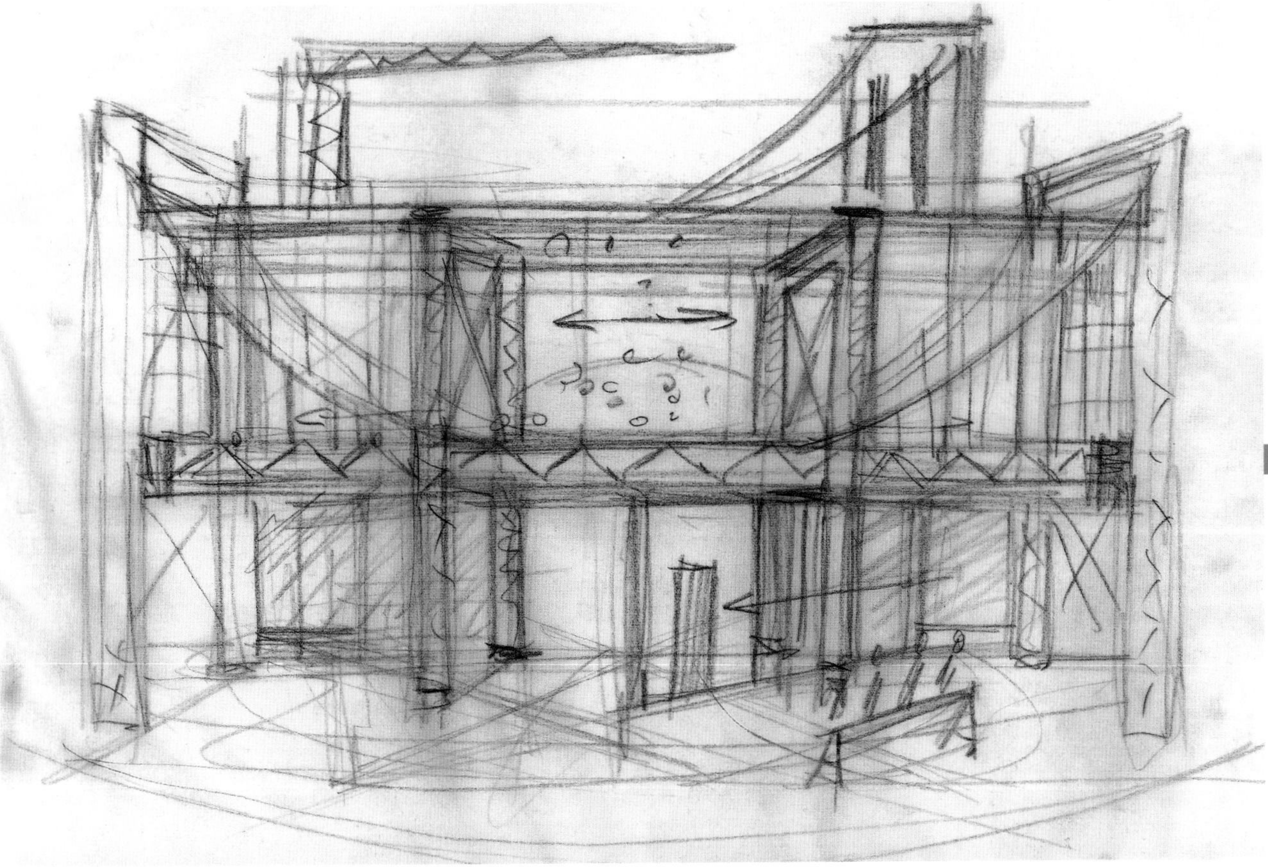

"There's that moment—the 'Oh' moment—when you suddenly look at your sketch and see, 'That's what it is'."

I also write notes to myself: "Openwork steel." And when you're working on something about New York, all you have to do is go outside and the thing you were thinking about pops out at you. It's like being in love—suddenly you're only looking at this one kind of architecture. And everything that's openwork steel makes an alarm noise, and you forget about the brownstones, you forget about everything else.

On the beauty of rough sketches

The rough sketches are the most beautiful things, because they have energy and thought. It's like looking at the cartouches of the Renaissance, the sketches that are off in the corner—they are so much more beautiful than those giant, mannered paintings hanging in the Louvre. The funny thing is that here I am drawing a drawing, and I don't even see what it is yet. And there's that moment—the "Oh" moment—when you suddenly look at your sketch and see, "That's what it is."

One of these drawings had a blue sky because you're looking through the structure in the park, and it's summer time. You know that you're going to be seeing through metalwork to the blue. So I'm working with negative-positive space. I put the blue in so that I can see the negative space better.

The story takes place in the day and then it goes to night. It's both. It's a 24-hour show. And here I am drawing some more—there are big billboards. And there's this big structure here. Then there's sort of this curvy thing around here. Like a bridge almost. It sort of looked like a train station for a while. Query "Bridges?" But I didn't know what it was, and then finally the idea came: it's a big, Forties' jazz band sitting on a bridge. And the bridge brings in all the scenery, and the dances are happening in and around it. Under the scenery, the bridge becomes a subway, and it becomes a museum, and it becomes Coney Island, and it becomes all these things.

This was the first time I'd worked with George Wolfe. I will show Peter Sellars an old Kleenex because he knows how to read it. With someone new, you're feeling each other out, so I actually did a rough model of a bridge with a band on it, and I showed him all this and he loved it. As many sketches as you see here, sometimes I make as many models. I have to work it all out in 3D.

I don't use much color when I design. Mostly the color comes later. Some people start with color. For me, color is a confusing issue that needs to come further along. Most often I will paint the finished model and that's where color comes in—but not always.

Likes and dislikes

I'm totally architectural. You know what I hate? Scenery. I like painting. I like photography. And I like architecture and sculpture. I am interested in volume and space. A lot of my scenery is about what's not there. What the negative is. And often stuff that moves around a lot—you don't even know what it's going to do until you see it on stage. Then it creates a whole new series of images, which represents a whole new level of discovery for everybody. Oh my God, it does that? *L'Allegro, il Penseroso ed il Moderato* for Mark Morris was like that. And then my sets come alive when there are people on them, because they are all about the proportion of the figure to the space.

Now I prefer music and opera to theater. For the first 15 years of my career I was doing many, many plays, new plays—Beth Hanley, John Shanley, Harry Kondoleon, John Robin Baites—and I found music in their language. However, many new plays are written like screenplays. And so often all you are doing is figuring out how to move the sofa on and off. It's prop, prop, prop, prop, prop. So it's more like a chore. Every now and again you hear a play that has really fantastic language in it. And then it conjures up its own images and its own music. And then you can approach it in the same way that you approach an opera.

Dr. Atomic,
John Adams and Peter Sellars.
San Francisco Opera, USA, 2005. Directed by Peter Sellars.

Dr. Atomic,
John Adams and Peter Sellars.
San Francisco Opera, USA, 2005. Directed by Peter Sellars.

"A good design—and it can be a multi-set or a single set—is one that takes on significance and that resonates at the end of a show."

Important influences

I went to graduate school. I was fairly young, but I had been working a lot already. I was lucky to get into a class with other very professional kids. Very ambitious and talented kids. I had a lot of the craft down already. I had been working as a draftsman in Hollywood for two years, and I'd assisted designers in New York. So I was really primed to be at Yale, because Yale was about developing one's conceptual ideas.

Ming Cho Lee really helped teach me a process. You make it your own as you go along, but he was a very good teacher that way. He was also frustrating and infuriating, and had his own way of doing things, and certainly a very strong aesthetic. So you were constantly battling that—and that's exactly what Ming wanted. You know, the strong students battled him and won. He was there so that you could find your own voice. I'm sure any great teacher does the same. And when you came in with a breakthrough design, he was the first to get excited. "Oh, wow!" he said. He loved ideas. He also loved good drawing.

Other great influences included my father, who was a well-known writer and illustrator of children's books; and a number of painting teachers. And I'm a great deal self-taught, too. I would take myself to Europe when I was 17 or 18 years old with 400 dollars that would last four weeks. And I'd photograph, and look and look and look. And this is what students aren't doing so much anymore: going to museums, looking at architecture, looking at what the sizes of buildings really are. Learning the difference between classical and neo-classical and baroque. All that stuff I taught myself.

Other big influences in my life? The pop artists, when I was little girl. I loved Oldenburg, Calder, Lichtenstein, Jasper Johns. You know, I was lucky. I grew up in New York and I was exposed to everything, and when I was 12 or 13 I started oil painting and of course I was obsessed with Degas and Manet and Monet and the Impressionists. It's only recently that I got to understand Van Gogh. He's so popular that I sort of pooh-poohed him. But actually he's one of the greatest painters who ever lived. Rembrandt: you look at his paintings and just weep. And when you look at one of those portraits, the person could be in the room with you. They're totally contemporary, those portraits. You see into someone's soul. It doesn't matter that they were painted in 1640. And that's what great art is.

I love the early Italian Renaissance. It's a very big influence in my work. Giotto and Piero della Francesca, Fra Angelico—pure geometry. I love Balthus, who was influenced by those people. I love Hopper, I love Birchfield. I love the Americans. It is very important to know enough about art and art history and architecture, where that stuff is coming from a deep place. So that you're not just flailing about because you have no reference point.

Working with other design elements

You work hand-in-hand with the lighting designer—you have to. If the lighting designer doesn't have a place to put his or her lights, your set's not going to look very good. And I've worked with some wonderful lighting designers. For example, when I know I'm working with James F. Ingalls, I know what he can do and I know how little there needs to be on stage for him to do it. And how flexible his work is. *L'Allegro*, *The Hard Nut*, all the Mozarts with Peter Sellars, *Nixon in China*, *Dr. Atomic*, *American Tragedy*, all the major works—it's Jim.

A good design—and it can be a multi-set or a single set—is one that takes on significance and that resonates at the end of a show. It needs to unfold and take on meaning, and become imbued with emotion and importance; it needs to connect with the piece in a way that keeps surprising, and that keeps allowing the audience to have ideas and revelations as the evening goes on.

Biography

Adrianne Lobel graduated from the Yale School of Drama at the age of 23 and began to work as a stage designer. Her Broadway credits include *A Year with Frog and Toad*, directed by David Petrarca; *On the Town*, directed by George Wolfe; *The Diary of Anne Frank*, directed by James Lapine; and *Passion*, directed by James Lapine. Among her opera sets for US and international companies are *Dr. Atomic*, San Francisco Opera; *An American Tragedy*, Metropolitan Opera; *Lady in the Dark*, Royal National Theatre, London; *Platée*, Covent Garden, London; *The Rake's Progress*, Châtelet Opera, Paris; and *Street Scene*, Houston Grand Opera. Her dance credits include *An American in Paris*, New York City Ballet; *Swan Lake*, Pennsylvania Ballet; *The Hard Nut*, Théâtre Royale de la Monnaie, Brussels; and *L'Allegro, il Penseroso ed il Moderato*, Théâtre Royale de la Monnaie, Brussels. She has received the Lucille Lortel Award, Obie Award, Long Wharf's Murphy Award, Joseph Jefferson Award, Emmy Award, a Tony nomination (for producing), Drama Desk nomination, Fany nomination, Maharam and Helen Hayes nominations, and the Prague Quadrennial Gold Medal.

Santo
Loquasto
Set and
Costume
Design

If, for many set designers, costume design is of equal importance, then Santo Loquasto is the perfect designer, because he does both. Theater, opera, and film—he has a mastery not only of the three-dimensional space, but also of the world of colors and the color palette. Here he discusses the advantages of being able to do costume and set design, as well as the importance of color in design.

Faust, Charles Gounod.

Metropolitan Opera, Lincoln Center, New York, USA, 2004. Directed by Andrei Serban. Set and costume design by Santo Loquasto. Faust and Mephistophales in the final moment of Faust *(Act V). Mephistophales holds an hourglass to show Faust that his time is up. Note the trapdoor used to create different stage levels.*

Introduction

Coming from the theater to opera and then cinema, Santo Loquasto is unique in that he has the ability to design for both Shakespeare and Woody Allen, who are worlds apart. It takes a skilled designer to address both. He is able to combine the needs of an architectural set with those of clothing the characters who inhabit it: what the characters wear is never independent of the spaces they inhabit. Being able to design both sets and costumes enables him to create a specific universe that combines shapes, colors, and forms to tell the story.

In this interview Loquasto talks about his design for *Faust*, a tragedy that, by definition, requires a demonic presence: dark shapes, forms, and overtones. Beyond answering with architectural shapes and forms, Loquasto also answers with color to create atmosphere and serve as a light counterpoint to the dark that is demanded by the tragedy.

Faust, Charles Gounod.

Metropolitan Opera, Lincoln Center, New York, USA, 2004. Directed by Andrei Serban. Set and costume design by Santo Loquasto. Model showing the tree in the middle of the garden (center stage) and the house on the right (Act II).

Faust, Charles Gounod.

Metropolitan Opera, Lincoln Center, New York, USA, 2004. Directed by Andrei Serban. Set and costume design by Santo Loquasto. Marguerite in the garden (Act II).

Approach

My starting point varies, depending on the play. I've been working lately with the Stratford Festival, in Canada, designing *As You Like It* on their stage. They're cutting back, so they don't want to change their stage, which is the one that Tyrone Guthrie and Tanya Moiseiwitsch designed in the Fifties—it's very much a throwback. When we did *Love's Labour's Lost*, a few years ago, I changed it, by making it essentially a rectangle. It was very simple and I thought it sat nicely in the space. However, there have been severe financial cutbacks, affecting the size of crews and changeovers, so they're asking us to use the space as it exists. You can take out certain elements, but I'm still toying with how to enliven it for an audience.

Knowing the play, having done it a couple of times, and knowing where I was doing it—these factors all influence the way I think. I also consider what's happening in the season and what the rep is like. I thought it would be fun to do *As You Like It* and settle on a period, because the costumes are the strongest contributory visual element, in a way. So you sort that out, and you look at the financial limitations, and then you try to figure out what you can do.

In *As You Like It*, there's a need to transform the space for the forest. That's the whole trick of it. You either do nothing, or you do something. You can't do a lot in that space, so the philosophy is to poke about and find whether (if you're setting it in the 1960s) you can make not a recreation of Woodstock as it was, but draw on the imagination of that time and place. In a way, you want it to be authoritative. You don't want it to be upsetting, but when you enter the theater, you want to invite the audience into a situation other than what they are accustomed to. Another time you might want to create a design that you simply want to be like a welcoming home. It's a very particular approach—or the beginning of an approach—because of the physical and financial situation.

On working for the Met

When I went to the Met to do *Faust*, everything was different. I met the director Andrei Serban first, and he talked about a number of things—but we had very little time. He talked about what he wanted in each scene, to a certain degree, but not how to get there or how to approach it. Just the elements that he felt were necessary.

Opera gets to be very complicated, and *Faust* is the reason I've never been interested in doing opera. I didn't want to get involved in traditional operas with specific expectations that I would be encumbered by. But here I am, and my reservations were well founded. They say, "No, no, no, you've got to have this, and you have to have that!" You're hamstrung. Especially in a big house, where they have an audience that comes expecting to know where they are, raised on a tradition of lush Italian design—Zeffirelli being, of course, the main proponent of this style, but others too. You look at the German productions, the Günther Schneider-Siemssen productions, and they have a different dynamic to them.

We talked about *Faust* being set in the 19th century, in Gounod's period, as opposed to medieval. It would have this sort of demonic presence throughout it, which is hardly surprising, and it would use certain elements in a sort of miniature human scale, instead of an operatic scale. Andrei has always worked in this kind of parallel activity. There's the narrative action of the text, and then around it is this reinforced activity; dumb shows or images. He did it in *Cherry Orchard*, and in *Agamemnon*. It's a favorite device of his.

The Met, however, did not want any of that. It has been an ongoing struggle, but the Met has bought into some of it, because I think we can make it quite beautiful. Andrei had such big ideas about how to do certain things physically that, within their rep, I could never offer him a solution that was feasible. You know they set up these productions in three or four hours. They can do certain things, because the theater has the machinery to do them, but you can't do everything. It's not like a Broadway show, which takes weeks in the theater to set up and operate.

It's also always interesting to know the traditions, if you look them up. To see what Peter Brook did with *Faust*, and what Rolf Gérard did with *Faust*, and what Harold Prince did with it—and Peter Stein. Sometimes you have to make choices and you just have to decide for yourself what it is that you like and don't like, regardless of who has impressed you.

When I did *Salome* with Jürgen Flimm, we met and talked, and I brought with me some books about architecture. We settled on a beginning. Then we went our separate ways, with Jürgen being in Germany and me being here, and the Met saying, "No, no, no, you should do this!" My studio did an enormous amount of work and we threw it all out when Jürgen came back and said, "No, I don't want this." He is very persuasive and has a solid history with the Met. And he knows how to handle them.

Faust, Charles Gounod.

Metropolitan Opera, Lincoln Center, New York, USA, 2004. Directed by Andrei Serban. Set and costume design by Santo Loquasto.

"It's how you connect with an audience and how you assault their senses or seduce them that interests me."

Faust, Charles Gounod.

Metropolitan Opera, Lincoln Center, New York, USA, 2004. Directed by Andrei Serban. Set and costume design by Santo Loquasto. Model of Faust in his study (Prologue).

Theater versus opera

I prefer to design for the theater. If the plays are good, they can be the most exciting, because they are human. Opera, when it works, can convey big emotion because it's reinforced by the sound and the music. It can be amazingly effective. The music is probably the biggest contributing factor, and that is what transports you—the sound. But theater is where my heart is.

I think many set designers want to do opera because of the scale: not only the monumentality of it, but the kind of impact that only that scale can give you. Working in my youth at the Delacorte Theater, in Central Park, gave me that opportunity in a way. It was inconsistently successful, but the scenery could be 36 feet high, and you felt that was a sort of cut-off height. And it could be fun. But again, how do you bring the audience into it and not have them look up at the jet-planes, or the fireworks, or the kids playing baseball 80 yards away? What I'm interested in is how to reach the audience. How do you touch them? It can be done on so many levels. It could be that they recognize the situation—you make the space physically familiar, and they're intimate with the space—or that the space is remote. It's how you connect with an audience and how you assault their senses or seduce them that interests me.

Combining costume and set design

Together, costumes and set punctuate the space. One reason I like to do both is that I can keep the color palette under control. Now, there are many collaborators who are more than willing to do that. I have had very happy relationships with many of them. But with others, I don't know what they are looking at. In a big production it's important for me to do it all, because I can organize the chaos of it.

With *Faust*, it was interesting. I always do the scenery first, but because we were so behind and the scenery kept changing, I started on the costumes. I have a wonderful long-time associate, Mitchell Bloom, and he went out and collected all these fabrics for me. It was a palette of textures, color, and scale. And having done *Luisa Miller* with him, I didn't want these costumes to fall into a rather generic 19th-century mire.

We looked at the film *Gangs of New York*, which is a mess, but is visually arresting and beautiful. And that was an influence on the whole production initially. I showed Andrei some pictures. It had physical spaces that worked for him, and I investigated incorporating that world, and that spirit and danger, into the world of *Faust*. There was something about the scale they used—very broad scales of plaids and bold patterns, which were often painted on people, because they were gangs and had their symbols.

I thought it would be interesting to push the scale of the patterns and to use color in the Kermis [the outdoor festival] in a rather extravagant way. They're still often rather muted colors, but there are very bold patterns and exaggerated shapes, which mimic the 19th-century photographs. Instead of making it tasteful and beautiful (which is very English, what I call the Merchant Ivory or Ralph Lauren solution), I chose to take a different route. The score is rather vulgar—in its lusciousness, let's say—and I would like to find a way to embrace that vulgarity, but with a point of view. It's a little more "in your face" than normal. It is, after all, a morality play and the change in costume tonality can underline that. Coupled with the difficulties inherent in designing *Faust* is the added issue of little time and a limited budget, and very complicated and difficult personalities, pulling you in many directions.

"Music plays a huge role in my design, and it's very important for me to keep music in mind."

Working with directors

I want to know what the director wants—if he has a sense of that—because that's what gives me the impetus to perceive, or to move on. I've designed now for a long time and I can function independently, but I prefer to collaborate.

I think American designers are often encouraged not to specialize or have too strong a personal style; to be chameleon-like and reflect the ideas of a director or choreographer. To serve the story exclusively. Now, that doesn't mean you're not asked to make a serious contribution. But you often work with directors who are not interested in competing with the scenery.

I've worked with the same choreographers for a long time—Twyla Tharp, Paul Taylor, and James Kudelka—each of whom is rather different. It's a question of how these people, who have a very particular way of seeing things, see the production. And it's how you can stay out of their way and contribute. Because of course you have to give the floor over to them. And that informs the way you work.

Complementing the score

Music plays a huge role in my design, and it's very important for me to keep music in mind. When I started working with Twyla Tharp, I went to a rehearsal and they danced a piece called *Sue's Leg*. A remarkable piece, in its time, and they danced it to a suite of Fats Waller songs, and I thought it was great. I asked Twyla about Fats Waller, and she said, "Oh, we're going to do it again for you, but to Brahms." She went on, "You can't let the music influence you; you have to respond to it in terms of the movement." So I went on and devised costumes that could work for both.

Often, when I work with Paul Taylor, he will send me the tape of the music before he starts choreographing. Sometimes I have ideas immediately about the kind of space that would apply: the degree of romance, the degree of energy I feel the space should have in it, and what they should wear … But this method now has the familiarity developed from the 30-something pieces I've done with him. The music is so much of an influence on the way I work that, when it was taken away from me, I had to really focus on the movement exclusively. It was extremely challenging.

Faust, Charles Gounod.

Metropolitan Opera, Lincoln Center, New York, USA, 2004. Directed by Andrei Serban. Set and costume design by Santo Loquasto. The end of Faust *(Act V), with Marguerite before a prison with inmates.*

I worked with Jerome Robbins on a handful of pieces—he was of, course, impossible to work with—but on the first piece, which was for Mikhail Baryshnikov and Natalia Makarova, he was anxious. As a result, it was the most eloquent piece I ever did for him. He was nervous, working with them, so he did not interfere in my work—I could design a very simple dress for Natasha and a tunic for Misha. It suited them, because I knew both of the dancers. It was very much like *Dances at a Gathering*, a continuation of what he had done. So I could draw on that. But it still had its own sweet identity in a way.

When I worked with Jerry on that most successful and popular piece, *The Four Seasons*, which is done to Verdi, it could really have been quite charming. It's quite popular at City Ballet, but City Ballet has its own kind of aesthetic. I was probably a little young, in terms of exposure, and Jerry doesn't really know how to work with designers, oddly enough, because designs in his productions have to be the way he wants them to be. But he doesn't really know what he wants, and he wants you to bring him endless choices—he's a shopper, I say. There are a lot of shoppers out there. You have to bring them 40 models and 200 sketches, and they're frustrated with your inability to complete their vision. There are a lot of those guys.

Designing Chekhov

A lot of spaces are simple. In *The Cherry Orchard* there was very little on stage. Andrei said, "I think there should only be on stage what it says in the script." So that was the beginning of it, and then came organizing the space, deciding it should all be white. At the time, I was unaware of Giorgio Strehler, and of the fact that he had done this beautiful production—a production even more beautiful than ours. Well, ours didn't look like the Strehler production, because the Strehler was at the Piccolo and we were at the Beaumont. As Woody Allen says, "Our own inadequacies will spare us comparison."

I had done a couple of other productions of Chekhov. I had worked with Nikos Psacharopoulos and he, regardless of his conventions, really understood the plays, and his sense of Chekhov's world was very informed. The way he approached designing for the emotions and actions of any play helped me as a young designer, and has stayed with me always. It's a kind of investment: it's about a theatrical moment, about fulfilling the potential of a theatrical situation. This is probably as much a part of what I try to do as anything. And I credit Nikos with it being such a big deal. There are all kinds of unknowns on stage. But the potential comes from the text. Or the music. If it's an opera, there are two things: the text and the music.

On Beckett versus Shakespeare

I don't think I've done any Beckett, but it would be exciting to design *Waiting for Godot*. More so even than *Hamlet*, because I think *Hamlet* is less mysterious. I never saw Liviu Ciulei's production, but I thought that making a banquet for the mad scene was marvelous. That's the whole thing about understanding physicality and how to create a scene where disruption is so embarrassing. That is really brilliant. *Hamlet* has its own set of problems, but *Godot* is harder. And *Hamlet* is so big. It would depend on where you're doing it, too. If you were doing it at Stratford …

Ming Cho Lee did a *Godot* up there in another space, in one of their other smaller theaters. There was this production that Mike Nichols did, and it was just silly-looking. It was all the things in the text rendered in this way that was amazingly realistic-looking and awful—and I was shocked. It had none of the heartbreak of the dilemma. Maybe it was actually very smart, but I didn't get it. No wit. No pain.

Beckett gives you absolutely no clues, but that's a good thing—it's liberating. It's like being given a free rein, and there are so many choices. You leap!

Biography

Santo Loquasto is a designer for theater, film, dance, and opera, and has won Tony and Drama Desk Awards for his set design for *Café Crown* and for his costume design for *The Cherry Orchard* and *Grand Hotel*. He received Tony nominations for his set design for *That Championship Season*, *What the Wine Sellers Buy*, *The Cherry Orchard*, *American Buffalo*, *The Suicide*, *Long Day's Journey Into Night*, and *Glengarry Glen Ross*, as well as for his costume design for *Ragtime* and *Fosse*. He has collaborated with Woody Allen on more than 24 films. Loquasto's costume designs for Woody Allen's *Zelig*, and his production design for *Radio Days* and *Bullets Over Broadway*, received Academy Award nominations. Other film work includes *Big* and *Desperately Seeking Susan*. Recent designs include *Movin' Out*, on Broadway and on tour, and *Salome* and *Faust* at the Metropolitan Opera. In 2005 he was inducted into the Theater Hall of Fame.

Jennifer Tipton

Lighting Design

If lighting design can be called an "art," then Jennifer Tipton has mastered the art to the point of being able to create a space for diverse productions, ranging from the avant-garde Wooster Group, with its multi-layered spaces and narratives, to the classical stage, requiring sharp and elegant design for works such as *Hamlet* and *King Lear*. Here Tipton discusses her approach to and process of lighting design, stressing the fact that the design is not finished until it is seen in conjunction with the production.

Introduction

Hamlet, William Shakespeare.
Yale School of Drama, New Haven, Connecticut, USA, 2003. Directed by Benjamin Mosse.

Jennifer Tipton is considered one of the world's finest lighting designers. Give her any text and space, and she will know how to design the lights for it. With such a degree of success, what is her secret? The answer is all too simple: for her, form follows content; whether it's a classic such as *Hamlet*, an avant-garde piece, a dance piece with one body and a video screen, an opera, or a contemporary theater-of-image piece, the play is the important starting point. Following this, her designs are based on the stage, the space, and the direction.

The search continues as her design is shaped on paper, with a plot, in the space of rehearsal and in the performance. Sometimes it takes until opening night (or closing night) before a lighting design is complete; sometimes the search continues as different productions illuminate the text and complete the answer. In this interview, Tipton discusses her process, philosophy, and approach to lighting design. For her, it is through the process of designing the production that the text shows its meaning and is understood.

As You Like It, William Shakespeare. *Yale Repertory Theatre, New Haven, Connecticut, USA, 1994. Directed by Stan Wojewodski Jr.*

"The three days that I spend at the drafting board, working on the plot using the drawings of the set, establish a great conversation with the set designer."

Approach

Talking about how you design is very difficult, because it is best communicated by your design and not by words, but I will try to go through the steps. The first thing you do is read the play in order to talk about it with the director, the set designer, and other designers, but you must leave it open. If I were to say, "I want this scene this way and that scene that way," and along came the director with his own ideas, I might say, "The way I wanted to light it doesn't work at all." So you read the play, have a strong, clear image of it, but leave it open for others involved to affect the way you think about it.

In some wonderful cases, the director will call everybody together at the beginning when no one has decided anything. That doesn't happen very often. Usually the design of the set is pretty much finished when the lighting designer is asked to come into the process, and that's sad, because there are things to be done at this stage. If the set is not finished, I may say, "Look at this wall—don't you think that if it were moved upstage a bit, or opened up, we could get lights in there." If the model is finished, I'm not going to go knocking a hole in the wall, in the same way that I wouldn't knock a hole for lights in the set on stage. So I just keep my mouth shut at this point, and try to light the play with what I've been given.

The three days I spend at the drafting board, working on the plot using the drawings of the set, establish a great conversation with the set designer. At the end of that time I really know what's going on in the set designer's mind and heart. I wish there were some equivalent device that would stimulate the same conversation with the director. Directors are very good with words, but sometimes it's hard to understand what those words really mean.

Working with directors and set designers

The designers and director often don't get together in the beginning because everybody is so busy. Even if you're in the same town, people are working here and there, and no one can get together at the same time. You're lucky to have one meeting. I have done productions after only a brief conversation with the director on the telephone. It's not the best way, needless to say.

I was doing a production of *The Magic Flute* and the producing opera company in Brussels flew me from New York all the way to South Africa to spend four whole days with the director/set designer. It was wonderful to spend so much time at such a seminal point. He [William Kentridge] is an artist; his conception of the production is total.

"I feel that each production has its light language, and I have to discover what that is."

Hamlet, William Shakespeare. *Yale School of Drama, New Havens, Connecticut, USA, 2003. Directed by Benjamin Mosse.*

My ideas have to work on the set; in the space I'm given. But my ideas are generally about the people of the play. It's also about discovering the style of the production. That generally comes from the director. The set designer will usually have spent a great deal of time developing the space with the director, so information about the style may flow through the set designer to me. And the style—rarely is something truly naturalistic put on stage; usually it's abstracted in various ways. How the light is abstracted is a choice that I will make at some point in the process. I may know immediately, or it may be that while I'm working on the plot the idea comes to me over time.

I like working with people who are risky. I've worked with JoAnne Akalaitis, Elizabeth LeCompte, Richard Jones, and these are directors who I find really stimulating. One of the things they all have in common is that they are "creatures." They are not thinking out what they are doing—it's an expression of what's in them in some way. Working with them is like a discovery, a journey. And that's what theater is after all; it's not just the play on the page, it's the ideas of the people who are putting it on the stage.

Using color

One of the last things I do is choose color. I will know certain things from the beginning. If there are night scenes and day scenes, it will probably mean that I need two sets of colors—one for each time of day. Or it may be more abstract than that. I may have ideas about source and shadow, or light and dark. It may be that I think about using colored light like paint, and therefore it should be more saturated.

I did a piece in Paris. A friend of mine saw it and said, "You're playing with the iris of the eye. You're not painting with light—it's more thought out than that. And more abstract than that." I think he was right in that case, a dance for the Paris Opera Ballet. I love to paint with color, but it's not every production that calls for that kind of painting.

Finding the light language

The thing I care about in particular is that the light in each production reflects the style of the production; and that I'm not repeating myself. I don't do things because that's the way I do them; I do things because I feel it needs to be done that way in that particular situation. And I'm very, very lucky because I work across the spectrum: from downtown theater groups like the Wooster Group to opera on the grand scale, and everything in between—dance, theater. Most lighting designers are pigeonholed. I think one of the reasons that I function so well across the spectrum is because my light reflects the needs of each particular production. I am thrilled to be learning new things all the time.

For instance, the first time I worked with the Wooster Group, I knew that they were "anti-theatrical," so I set about trying to find a new vocabulary for the light. Designing lights for the Wooster Group and their *Poor Theater* represents such a dichotomy. I certainly thought of doing it with as few lights as possible. But the equipment: great big screens facing the audience; very pretty, expensive items. It's all a crazy world ...

I feel that each production has its light language, and I have to discover what that is. Devising the plot is establishing that language. When I go into the theater to make the cues, then I'm using that language—the words—to make sentences and paragraphs and meaning. I do feel that lighting has a meaning separate from the content of a production. Obviously it has to make the story clear, otherwise the audience will be confused. But there is the story of the light as well.

I think of light as music for the eye. It can lead an audience fluidly from one place to another, from one feeling to another. It has structure and rhythm. You establish a theme, and then make a variation on that theme. It tells you where to look; it tells you how to feel about what you see.

What you find is that if you leave something over there—a detail, or a person standing—if you leave them in the dark, that calls attention to them. If you brush them with a little bit of light, they become part of the picture; the focus goes back to the focal point. It's about composition. But then you also need to know how the focus changes. For the audience to comprehend it all, there needs to be a focal point. It may be tacit, but it is certainly worked out in concert with the director. Sometimes I find that the director may disagree and want the emphasis somewhere else, but generally I find that I intuitively know where it should be.

Teaching lighting design

At Yale, I teach my process. We read the play, then we do what I call a "conceptual hook-up"—that is, a list of what the play needs with respect to light. Then we look at the set and decide where the possibilities are for placing lights. We take our list and look at the space, and then we go back and forth between these two things until finally the list represents what the play needs, in the context of what is possible. In the beginning the list may be longer than the dimmers that we have, or may represent more equipment than is available in the theater. I always like it when you have to cut back, because it means you'll be economical in the end. In the process of going back and forth between the space given and the ideas developed from discussions with everyone involved, you can make the final list and do the plot—that is, develop the light language of the play. And hopefully it's the right language.

There have been times when I've discovered that I misunderstood; that I felt I did not have the wherewithal to light the play. I did not have the lights hanging in the necessary places or in the necessary color. Too often I've gotten into the theater and haven't had the lights to make the first look. How could I have missed it? In that case I add them. But there isn't the time to rehang totally. Having the wrong light language can be devastating for a production. You have to be particularly careful with a new play that has no track record; it may be its only chance. If the lighting is wrong, the audience and critics are going to blame the play, not the lighting designer.

When I read the play, I see the people in the light. And I think the light should come from different angles: maybe I feel the light should come from a low angle to make the actors strange-looking; or that it should be a bright sunny day, if it's going to be naturalistic. Or perhaps there should be an HMI [Hydrargyrum medium-arc iodide, a mercury halide discharge short arc lamp] that washes the whole landscape with a brutal kind of light—the light I imagine speaks my feelings about the play and the people in it.

I love stimulating young people. And I don't feel that I'm a teacher—I'm a provocateur, if you like. They're there for three years, six semesters. The first semester I teach them how I do it. From then on I try to stimulate them to find the way they do it.

I do find myself mentoring students. There are two students taken into the lighting program each year at Yale, so there are only six in the school at any time. It's great; it's a very individual relationship. After they graduate I have them come to the studio one morning a week and pay them a little bit of money, just so that they have a home, as it were, when they're trying to get their feet on the ground. If I hire them as an assistant, if I hire them to draft, then I pay them the going rate.

Electric Haiku, Cathy Weis.
Dance Theater Workshop, New York, USA, 2005. Choreographed by Cathy Weis.

"Light can transport you in the same way that music can."

Favorite experience

The experience that immediately comes to mind occurred in the early Seventies, very early in my life. It was a group of pas de deux, classical ballet pas de deux, put together by Jerome Robbins in Spoleto, Italy, for the Festival of Two Worlds. He put a procession of five couples in the beginning of the piece, and at the end he put together parts of each couple's *Swan Lake*, white-swan pas de deux, which made a very beautiful closing. There was something right about the air, the situation.

Dance does have a script: it has its beginning, middle, and end. It has form. It's all about structure. I'm very formal as a person as well as an artist. That's why I love working with Trisha Brown, because she is so formal in her thinking about the structure of the dance. It isn't that you just put light on the stage. There are ways of thinking about dance that guide your structure—a beginning, a middle, and an end. I tell my students that I often find when the curtain goes up on a dance that there are dancers standing in a pool of light; the music begins; the pool of light goes away and the dancers dance on the whole stage. The curtain comes down and we've never seen the pool again. To me, that pool is the statement of a theme in light. You then develop that theme. If it's there only because it's the one time that the dancers are standing still, it is superfluous to the lighting in general.

The rhythm of the light

What we see first in the light is always very important. It needs to be something organic and integral to the composition of the light in the piece. And that's so for every production. It also helps the audience when things get complicated. If the lighting is well structured, it helps them to remember the beginning when they get to the end.

Light is music for the eyes—it can transport you in the same way that music can. And it follows the same rigorous rules. I sense it very strongly. I know that when you see a production of a play with a lot of little scenes, the rhythm of the light can make you feel that the play is endlessly long or just the right length. The rhythm of the play is made by the changing light. When I light a play, when I spend time with it in that way, I can begin to understand it. I can't get at plays from reading them alone—I have to light them in the theater itself, after plotting the lights. That's when I really get to know a play, when I'm living with it in the theater. And that includes some previews, so that it incorporates the audience. Not that I react to their response, but it affects me. I'd certainly change something at that point if the story wasn't being made clear by the light, or by the production team; and if the lights can help, I will certainly change cues or color or timing. Just being in the audience and feeling how they respond makes a difference. Part of me says I'm not affected by the audience; that this is my work, and it is what it is. But the other part knows that the audience is part of the work, and if we did the production without an audience, it would never be complete.

On Beckett versus Shakespeare

I'd light *Waiting for Godot* in the same way I'd light *Hamlet*. I would make a list of the needs. Because it's an enigmatic play, because Beckett is Beckett, it would make me feel in certain ways, and I would try to figure out how I would express those feelings in light. I have a visceral response to a play.

I'm interested in doing *Lear* because I don't understand it. I understand *Hamlet* very well. I have done since college, when I wrote a paper on it. I understand most of good ol' Will's plays, but that one I don't—that one is bleak, that one is Beckettian. So I'd just love to get in it and wander around for a bit. Each play has a lot to do with feelings. There is one person—the brain and the heart are one.

There's something I respond to in a play, and I want the audience to respond. I feel very strongly about that. It's a balance. I want the audience to respond viscerally, and yet I don't want to make it so specific that they have only one way to respond. Take a play

Electric Haiku, Cathy Weis.
Dance Theater Workshop, New York, USA, 2005. Choreographed by Cathy Weis.

Electric Haiku, Cathy Weis.
Dance Theater Workshop, New York, USA, 2005. Choreographed by Cathy Weis.

like *Waiting for Godot.* I don't want to indicate to the audience that this is the way you are supposed to feel, this is what the play is about. The play happens to be about not knowing. It really is about translating my gut reactions into the light on stage, but allowing room for the audience's gut reactions as well.

The emotional needs of the play may have to do with the color, or with the tempo of the cueing. Sharp changes may elicit a certain response from the audience; they may wake them up or warn them about something that is about to happen. It's not that I'm manipulating the audience; it's that I'm showing them the landscape of this event. Manipulation is a kind of button pushing, and there are many theater people who do that. Of course it's possible to do it with lights. You put everything in a golden glow...

Background

I came to New York to be a dancer. I danced for a few years with a company called the Merry-Go-Rounders. Then I became rehearsal mistress for the Merry-Go-Rounders. Our director, Lucas Hoving, was a choreographer himself and didn't want to see every performance. As assistant rehearsal director, I went to every performance in order to critique the dancers. I looked at the bigger picture—and that was light. I fell in love with light and I've been in love with light ever since. I always manage to look at the bigger picture, which is why I'm successful at what I do. It's always the context—it's how we see what we see.

I did not go to any school; I went out on the road with Paul Taylor. One big opener for me was Jerome Robbins' *Celebration: the Art of the Pas de Deux.* That production—not only do I remember it as something special, but other people remember it as well, and it brought me a lot of work. That was my break. But I learned lighting on the road with Paul Taylor. I learned the craft. And it was great—I think that's a wonderful way to do it. You have these ideas and put them on the stage, and then you say, "Ugh, how terrible, it doesn't work at all." Now in ordinary circumstances you'd be stuck with it, and you couldn't change it, but being on tour, you can go to a different theater the next night, change the whole thing if you want, and hang lights differently. You have the time, you're going from theater to theater, you can redo the whole thing each time, rather than being stuck in one place for a three-week run, where you have to live with your mistakes.

As for music, as a lighting designer I don't have a preference. My parents were very Victorian: my father adored Dickens, my mother adored Thackeray, and we listened to Wagner all the time. And when I went to college I was shot into the 20th century, and I fell in love with Bartók and Faulkner and Franz Klein. By nature, I like Shostakovich and Bartók, where there are tensions that unsettle the order, but recently I lit the da Ponte Mozarts, which I adored, and I'm working on *The Magic Flute.* My first opera—one of the first operas that I fell in love with in my life—was Stravinsky's *The Rake's Progress.*

On American versus European approaches

America's philosophy is that you use a lot of sources. Jean Rosenthal, for instance, had what she called "jewel" lighting—light that came from all angles in such a way that it looked as if the source of the light was the actor. In Europe, they have big lights that take up a lot of room on the pipes, so you can't have many of them. There is a sense of an outside source, rather than the actor being the source, as in America. It's difficult to impose my way of thinking about light on the European system. My way of seeing things is very American as well.

I did an opera at Covent Garden with a German director. He said, "This would never work in Germany. It's just much, much too beautiful." I asked in dismay, "Is it wrong, do you want me to change it?" And he said, "No, no, don't change it! But it wouldn't work in Germany."

Hansel and Gretal, Engelbert Humperdinck.

San Francisco Opera, USA, 2002. Directed by Linda Dobell.

I did *Peer Gynt* with Liviu Ciulei at the Guthrie, and *Hamlet* at the New York Shakespeare Festival, among others. I was a bit younger then; he was too. And he wanted to tell me what to do, and I was rather determined for him not to, because I knew I could do it much quicker than if we sat there together. In those days they gave Liviu what he wanted. We lit for hour after hour, night after night, sitting and looking at the lighting.

I do find the directors more interesting in Europe, though I don't get the opportunity to work with them that much. But for some reason they do theater that is more challenging.

The secret of good lighting design

Good lighting design is due to the composition, rhythm, appropriateness. Composition meaning how the lighting makes you look where you should look; how it controls all of that, both in space and in time. Rhythm: how it changes and how it breathes with the play. And appropriateness: to the material, to the content; whether the form is actually suiting the content of the play, or of the production. The play may be seen in different ways by different directors. Santo Loquasto, with whom I work quite a bit, says, "Where's the line between polish and slick?" And I walk that line. I polish a lot, and there are those times when it gets too slick, I'm sure.

Bill Forsythe is the best lighting designer in the world. I've known him since he was a kid. He's the best because he takes the materials and uses them. He uses his eyes in wonderful ways that are totally appropriate for the dance. I love his light. He knows what he's seeing. And he knows how to change it. I always say that Billy is the best. He says, "I saw what you were doing with those lights over there, and I thought, 'what is she doing?' So I put some lights over there and I turned them on." That's his approach. He's been in Germany, so he has these big lights there in his theater. He uses them better than anybody else whose work I've seen.

As for Bob Wilson, I worked with Bob for a while and he always does it the same way. And once I learned that way, then it was time to move on, because I like to learn different ways. I like to learn the right way for the moment, for what we're doing right now. And whatever Bob does, he does it the same way. It's very, very beautiful. Each element is wonderfully considered with a great deal of air around it—but it always looks more or less the same. When I worked with him he was designing through me, as he does with everybody—anybody. He does the part that he likes, and leaves the part that he doesn't like for other people.

The challenge of lighting

I definitely believe that lighting is complex, but I am known as someone who does not use many lights. It's simple in that respect, but I do feel that there is only one right place to put a light for a given purpose, and if you need it in two colors then you must compromise. Two lights cannot physically go in the one "right" place. One of my former students works on Broadway a lot now; he recently lit an August Wilson play with 500 lights. I haven't a clue what they were all for. If you put a gun to my head, I could not light an August Wilson play with 500 lights. For Ham and Clove, in *Endgame*, which I've done a couple of times, I think the challenge of gray light is such a conundrum. It's great to work on something like that. You can't say, "Audience, this is gray light," because you have to leave the conundrum in their head too. It's a great challenge.

I adore theater. To get in a room and image ourselves, what could be more thrilling. To do it well means that you have to be serious about it, that your reasons for doing it have to be right. It's always a challenge.

Biography

Jennifer Tipton is well known for her work in theater, dance, and opera. Her recent work in opera includes Tchaikovsky's *Queen of Spades*, San Francisco Opera, and Mozart's *The Magic Flute*, La Monnaie, Brussels. Her recent work in dance includes Paul Taylor's *Spring Rounds*, Lar Lubovitch's *Elemental Brubeck*, and Christopher Wheeldon's *Quaternary*, San Francisco Ballet in Paris; Trisha Brown's *O Composite*, Paris Opera Ballet; and Shen Wei's version of the Chinese Opera, *The Second Visit to the Empress*, at the American Dance Festival. In theater her recent work includes John Vanbrugh's *The Provoked Wife*, American Repertory Theatre, Cambridge, Mass.; *The Moon for the Misbegotten*, Long Wharf Theatre, New Haven; and *Poor Theater* for the Wooster Group. Tipton teaches lighting at the Yale School of Drama. She received the Dorothy and Lillian Gish Prize in 2001, the Jerome Robbins Prize in 2003, and the Mayor's Award for Arts and Culture in New York City in April 2004.

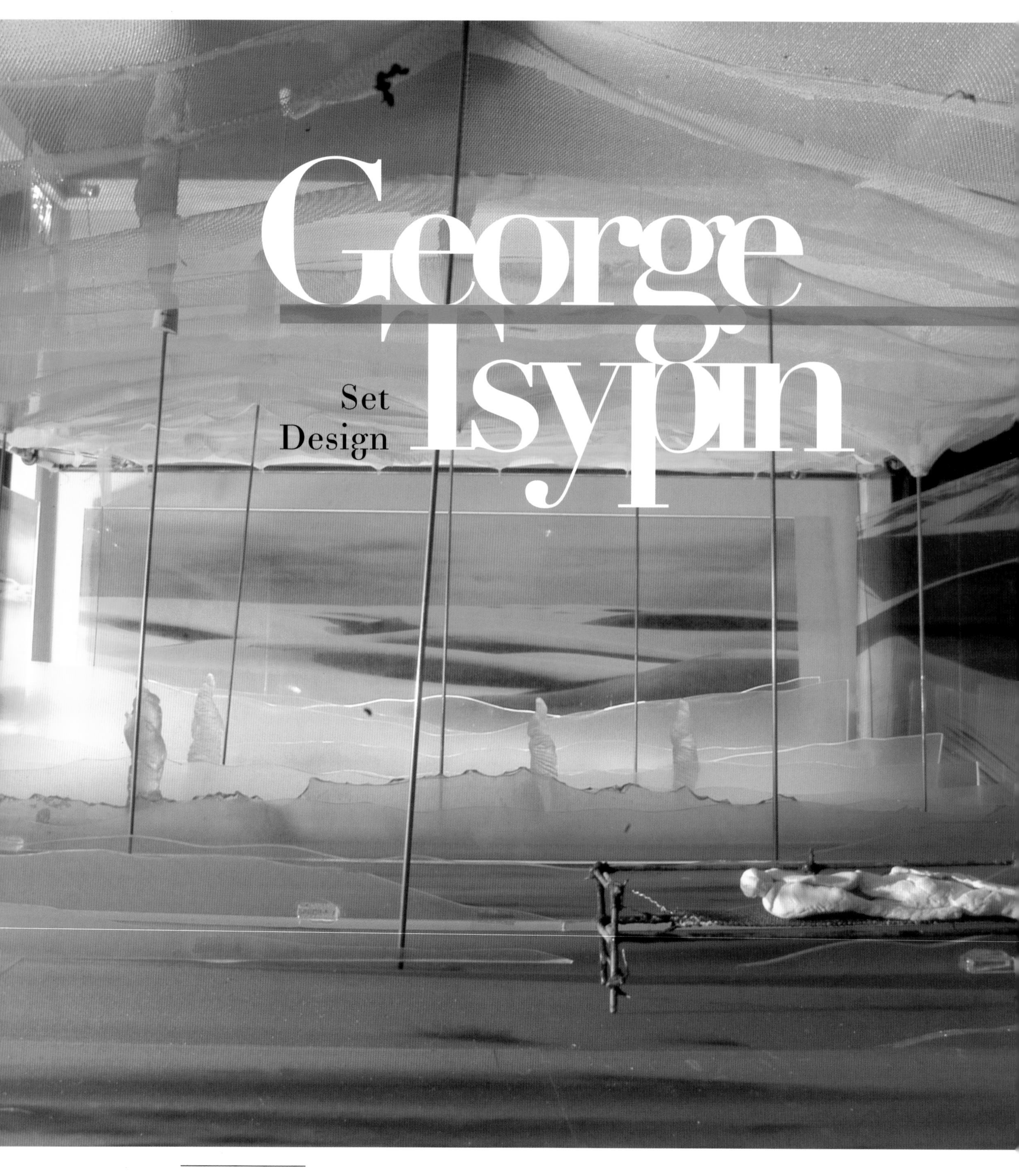
George
Tsypin
Set
Design

If sculpting space can be seen as a sculptor creating shapes in an architectural space, then this is second nature to George Tsypin. Both a sculptor and an architect, he uses the empty space as his stage and sculpts shapes and forms to fill and move within that space. Here he likens his job as a designer to that of a choreographer, where both are creating spaces for actors to move, dance, and act in.

Introduction

Waiting for the Barbarians, Philip Glass and Christopher Hampton. *Erfurt Theater, Erfurt, Germany, 2005. Directed by Guy Montavon. "Under undulating net, 17 scrims rising from the floor create visions of settlements in the desert."*

For George Tsypin, any play or opera is a good reason to design a set. How does he approach it, though? How does he design his spaces? How does he know how to sculpt to Wagner versus how to sculpt to Mozart?

In this interview he explains that it is partially the work of the music—the music will let you know how to move, just as it does with a choreographer—and partially the work of dreams. Regardless of the composer or the music, Tsypin's spaces are unique in that they almost all represent an architect's work and vision, along with that of a sculptor; he admits this to himself: that his designs are very much informed by his background and training as an architect.

Adriana Mater, Kaya Sarayaho. *Opera de Bastille, Paris, France, 2006. Directed by Peter Sellars. "The story of war, rape, and broken cycle of violence takes place in a vaguely Muslim village that could be former Yugoslavia, Chechnya, or Afghanistan."*

"I am waiting for the moment when I have an absurd vision or idea, or at least something that cannot be explained verbally. Then I begin to feel that maybe I am on the right track."

Approach

I wish I knew what my starting point is. What I mean by that is: if there was a mechanism and you knew how to start, that would help a lot. Unfortunately, every time you start from scratch. You start as if this is the first show you ever designed. That's the mystery. That's the struggle. But once you've found that starting point, the rest is easy. And ideally every time it's a different starting point.

On *The Magic Flute*, I went to sleep and while I was sleeping—or not, I'm not sure—I had the image of a magic crystal temple that was breaking at different parts and then reassembling itself like a kaleidoscope. The fragments defragmented and then rearranged themselves. And I sensed the possibility of different elements being used for different scenes. I had a feeling of Masonic architecture and I used a bit of that. And I thought that maybe the whole universe would be constrained in that temple, in a vague vision of a temple.

I wish I knew how this mechanism works, but designing is dreaming. It's exactly the same. It's just being able to be in that particular state at all times. That's what designing is. I don't know really how it works and why our creativity is connected to dreams. My suspicion is that it's the ability to unify when you're dreaming, as opposed to analyzing when you're breaking things apart. But it's also something else—through dreams we're connected to something, and I don't really know what that is.

You look at the text, you listen to the music. For quite a while you're trying to rationalize—you're searching in a rational way for a way to do a show, to try and envisage that particular opera or play. I am waiting for the moment when I have an absurd vision or idea, or at least something that cannot be explained verbally. Then I begin to feel that maybe I am on the right track. Often what I focus on is an actual object of the model. Sometimes I find that's a very useful creative device. You don't really design the show; you need to create a little object of that sculpture. It's sitting on the table, and that will eventually lead you to the show.

Let's say that I walk around in the woods and I see a beautiful rock. There is something exciting about the rock, and it suggests something to me. It's the reality of this particular rock that excites me, and that's maybe a future show right there.

What's important is that this object has a certain energy. You just have to trust the physical reality of this particular object. Let's say it's a piece of wood or glass, or the way this particular

glass reflects the light. Or the stone lying on the glass has got so much that, if you really look closely, the entire universe is encapsulated in this object—maybe the universe of this specific show. It resonates with thinking about that particular music or that particular atmosphere that you are trying to capture. And then all of a sudden there is this electrical charge. But it's not like you go around and find that. Often you have a whole group of people here. And that's what you're struggling with: we have to come up with that object. Hopefully it's a kinetic thing, and it has potential to transform.

The mystery doesn't get cracked open. You touch it—you encounter it. Or at least you discover a little door. You never enter that door, but at least you identify the door. My role is to identify the door. When you listen to opera, there is a world inside your head. And I see if I can bring that world to a live installation, but essentially you only have your own world in your mind. There is only that, and you just have to have the courage to make it happen.

The creative process

You read the play, and it triggers things in your own mind; the things you know, that excite you, and that resonate with your own world. And those are the only things you can realize on stage. You cannot do what you don't know. There are some things I have never seen. That is the limitation, and once you accept that, it makes you free. It is very scary because the point is that once you realize there is no Prokofiev, there is no Mozart, there is no Wagner … Maybe you listened to that music and it made your heart beat a little bit faster, but you are still doing your own thing. Whatever you do doesn't really relate to the music.

And that's why very often people hire visual artists and sculptors; the only difference is that they know in advance what they are going to get: that this artist will basically give them the same thing. But a designer is supposed to be more versatile and create a new thing every time, although it doesn't really work that way. I have to admit I am basically designing the same opera all the time.

Grendel, Elliot Goldenthal.

LA Opera and Lincoln Center Festival, USA, 2006. Directed by Julie Taymor. "Grendel, the monster, is standing by the miniature Meadhall. The Earth/Ice wall is a symbol of nature being ravaged by the advance of human civilization."

"I often find that when I know too much, it gets in the way. I need that distance."

I don't mean that in a bad way. I'm developing those ideas. There is always a little discovery. I am not saying I am stuck with the same set—they are always different sets. But you design one set and you discover something. And then it leads you somewhere else. It is an inward journey; a very personal journey.

Obviously there are practicalities. There is some logic in the story to which you respond, but that is not the most important thing. You can slap that on top, although that is not what you do. To me, it's similar to what composers do. When you say, "Before, you did *The Love for Three Oranges* and now you are doing *War and Peace*," that is a very different subject, and yet you recognize that composer right away because there is something about the music-making that is recognizably his.

On distance and rebellion

When you deal with opera, the greater the opera, the sillier the story. Sometimes the story suggests a place, but often it doesn't. Wagner doesn't really say where it is taking place; it is a universe very often. That is not a big help. I often find that when I know too much, it gets in the way. I need that distance. I need to know the libretto—people are saying this and this, and this kind of story is taking place—but I really should have my distance. It's best when I don't remember.

When I come to a new city, I don't really look, but I have an impression of that city. If you really look and take pictures, it doesn't get you close. It is maybe better to close your eyes and take it in, because you need to capture something else. It is similar when you design. When you really study the text, you get bogged down and it doesn't move you forward. When I do *Don Giovanni* for the fifth time, on opening night I read the subtitles and I am shocked. "Oh, that is what they are saying!" People make fun of me, but it is a strategy—it is not an accident.

Yes, I am being rebellious. The whole act of making theater is very rebellious … It's almost destructive. That is the essence of theater: you go against your own expectations. First of all you have to rebel against yourself, and that is what makes it so difficult—because if you have done it before, it has to be destroyed. The point is that you don't really need to design. Design is created and will always be destroyed.

Design is especially vulnerable because it is very material. And the essence of theater isn't material. You go to the theater because you need that immaterial experience. And all of a sudden there is a designer who has just built a wall, a piece of architecture. Do you know what the purpose of that is? It is to create a little movement with that wall in someone else's soul. It is not an easy task. This wall is not supposed to be there. The point is not the wall—the point is that little emotion or experience, the discovery that the audience member makes. I am very aware of this. I have nothing else. I have to work with the real materials in order to create an immaterial experience. We are going against the materials. For the composer or poet or playwright, it is a bit easier because they are already dealing with immaterial media. They don't work against themselves.

The second point is that there's Mozart who wrote this score, and it is written down and everyone comes and looks at the score and interprets it. Musicians interpret the score—and some of them do it very brilliantly. They look at the set, and of course they listen to the music, but they know the music already; they don't know what to expect on stage. But I come in, and I have my empty space. You say that the score helps, but it doesn't really because it is a completely different medium. I have to create from scratch; it's more immediate. So should I serve Mozart, or should Mozart serve me? Today, even at the Met, the audiences are all like children. Everyone wants visual entertainment. So am I going to sit at home and say, "This is Mozart, I should be careful?" No, I have my work to do.

The Ring Cycle, Richard Wagner. *Mariinsky Theatre, Saint Petersburg, Russia, 2003. Production concept by Valery Gergiev and George Tsypin. "Four giant figures, which represent primordial gods, are floating in the air. During the opera they morph into trees, fire, water, dragons, and semihumans. They follow the main protagonists, telling their own meta story."*

"I discovered that the further I went, and the stranger I got, the more people responded. That's the paradox. The more personal I got, the more people reacted."

Finding a personal approach

I never said I was against the text. I may be totally in tune with the text. All I am saying is that theater, and especially opera, is such a synthetic world. What's important is that it is the fusion of many different forms. All this pretension that this one form is somehow real Mozart—that is nonsense. Because who is there to judge? You hear Mozart and you see something in your head; somebody else sees something else.

On one of the early operas that I designed, I worked with a woman director who did *Lady Macbeth* by Shostakovich, while he was still alive. She directed the first production 40 years ago, which is now considered a classic. And then 30 years later I was asked to design for her, and she had a pack of letters from Shostakovich that said, "This is a perfect production." And she was running around with these 22 letters from Shostakovich, the premier composer of the 20th century, who said that this was the definitive production. Now I came in, and what did I do? I did what I usually do. I was trying to listen to the music and find my own personal approach—my own reaction. I had no idea how people would react, or what it looked like to somebody else.

I was a student at NYU, and I never planned on a professional career in theater. I felt, "I am still young, I should just explore," but I wasn't planning to be a set designer. I was simply interested in this particular medium and this world of imagination—that's what excited me. And then I thought, since I had nothing to lose, that I would do something I liked, something really strange. And I discovered that the further I went, and the stranger I got, the more people responded. That's the paradox. The more personal I got, the more people reacted. The more objective you get, the less people react.

I need to grow, and I'd like to grow. And I do grow, but whether I grow by designing more productions, I am not sure. Unfortunately, I feel as if it is definitely not enough. I feel that I grow more when I venture into other things.

We don't choose our themes. Themes are dictated by life. We are all exploring one thing, maybe two. And they are life and death, and maybe love. Do I come up with new themes? No.

West Side Story, Leonard Bernstein. *Bregenz Festival, Bregenz, Austria, 2003–2004. Directed by Francesca Zambello. "Designed six months before 9/11, this captures the nightmarish vision of a collapsing skyscraper. Situated in the middle of the lake, the image can be also be read as the Phoenix rising. There is a distant, forever unattainable, vision of Manhattan at the top of the structure."*

Working with directors

Why do I consider Peter Sellars such an important figure in my life? I was doing a gallery show, exhibiting my sculpture and drawings. And then I started working on a production with Peter. I started asking him questions, trying to be a good designer. How are you going to do this scene? How big is the chorus? And he just didn't want to discuss that. He said, "You want to be an artist? Be one." Of course you need brilliant directors to do something like that. I have been lucky. I know quite a few of them. They are smart. They know not to dictate in order to exploit my talent to the full, because then there is an interesting tension. But Peter was the first one to say, "Be an artist."

It is a very strange thing. I realized that I should not be directing the show when I am designing it. The further I get away from directing, the better my work becomes. When I give the director something completely impossible, then it becomes moderately interesting. When I try to get into the director's mind, it's as boring as hell.

When a form or space takes you somewhere, you should go there. When I see a show, I am thrilled because I never imagined this could be used in this way or that would work that way. That is the unpredictable happening, because the director comes in and all of a sudden it is something else.

Working without directors

In opera, in big productions, there is a slightly different rhythm—it is not like designing a play. Essentially, design is more important in opera. I started working with Valery Gergiev, the conductor and head of the Maryinsky Theater, who has a whole philosophy about directors not being important at all. He always says, "When we had this artist and that artist 100 years ago, everyone knows them, but nobody knows who directed those shows." Although, of course, at that time there were no directors.

He gave me so much freedom and so much responsibility that I moved into a position where I just have to conceive a visual world of the opera. And then, if a brilliant director comes in and does an amazing job, I'm lucky.

I feel I've changed gradually in the last 10 years—changed in the sense that, even at the Met, people expect that I take charge, almost. For example, I did the *Ring Cycle* in St. Petersburg and there was no director. Well, there was one, then there was another, and then there was an assistant and an assistant director. There were many, many people. There was a whole discussion, and Gergiev announced that he didn't need a director anymore. And that's an interesting question, and I'll tell you why. For example, in Wagner, the singers are so limited in

The Magic Flute, Wolfgang Amadeus Mozart.

Metropolitan Opera, Lincoln Center, New York, 2004. Directed by Julie Taymor. "The crystal temple represents an inner spiritual journey as you go through its vaults and arches. With trials by fire and water, you change your nature."

"My training in architecture is the most important thing in my work. My work has become more sculptural, but in essence I am an architect."

what they can do. The music is so complex, and what they have to do is so incredible, musically, that there are only so many options. They have to stand around, and deliver. So sometimes I feel that's all there is to it. There's a singer delivering his part, and musicians, and the design. Sometimes design carries the show. Not always—sometimes it can be a disaster as well. But opera almost always teeters on the verge of not needing the director.

In that *Ring Cycle*, I wanted to create sets that act like actors and move all the time. It didn't succeed, because you have to realize that people come and actually listen to the music, and the visuals have to go into the background. But ideally I'd like to create sets that are just as alive as the actors. Maybe one day that's the ideal for me. I'm trying to create playful sets, but of course there are big sections where nothing happens. But maybe there will be new technologies, whereby you can create something as elastic as a human being.

On the importance of form

I know that at Tisch School of the Arts, John Conklin is now teaching designers to be rooted very seriously in the dramaturgy of the text. What I actually got from John was something quite the opposite, which is that the design is an accident. He would just get on a chair, play with the set, move it—that's my main memory of John. That everything happens in that particular moment. In fact later on, when I was trying to grow as a designer, I felt that his approach was very different from my training; that, as a former architect, I am much more rigorous. I have to have form—there's nothing accidental. I don't mind the playfulness, but formally it wasn't as tight as I needed things to be, as an architect. Maybe I loosened up a bit. However, I still very much work around the form. I need everything connected like this.

That doesn't mean literally connected. Just everything working towards or around one formal approach—it's a poem that I'm writing, and it's tight. I can't stand it when something doesn't really connect to something else. When people just throw shapes together, or all of a sudden something just shows up on stage. I almost admire other designers that they can loosen up to such a degree. But the unity and integrity of the design are very, very important to me.

Nevertheless, that's what I admired about John. When he got on the stool and put something on somebody else's model upside down—for me, that was the key. What was important was that he trusted his own hand. His mind wasn't working at that moment. His hand simply went there and did everything, in just the same way a child plays. It's not about studying the text,

The Magic Flute, Wolfgang Amadeus Mozart.

Metropolitan Opera, Lincoln Center, New York, 2004. Directed by Julie Taymor.

although you need to study the text in order to get to that point. You don't exclude anything. Why would I exclude the words? Sometimes the word can spark an image. That is what's so beautiful.

Designing *The Magic Flute*

I have a long history with Julie Taymor [Director of *The Magic Flute*], and we now have a very good relationship. She is constantly criticizing my set, but in a friendly way. The set in *The Magic Flute* is very precise—in a way it's very architectural, even though there are a lot of abstract shapes. And Julie's work is soft, and that's why the set goes against her sensibilities so much, and she had to struggle with it. But in my mind that's what makes the show work: this combination of fluidity and softness that she brings to it, and the hard edge that I bring to it. And this is necessary for the scale of the Met, because I shape the space; it's always formed, and yet there's also this kind of fluid, feminine quality to it. And that combination is exactly what makes the show work.

The space where I'm designing doesn't really matter to me. I try to spend as little time as possible in the theater, because it's so depressing. No, your space is in your mind. There are locations where you have to deal with a particular situation, such as when I designed for the lake in Bregenz. Or when I did the *Ring* in Amsterdam, where the theater itself was transformed. Then of course you're aware of the architecture of the theater, but if you really decide you're confined to the empty void of that stage, then the world is the world.

My training in architecture is the most important thing in my work. My work has become more sculptural, but in essence I am an architect. I am still inspired by architecture.

On Mozartian and Wagnerian spaces

Designing for Mozart and Wagner is similar, but when you hear Wagner's music you move one way, and when you hear Mozart's music you move another way. That's exactly what the sets do. That's what happens to the space—it dances with the music, and it just dances in a different way. Or takes a different pose. In French it's called plastique.

Mozart and Wagner were both trying to create their own universe, and you can use any object you want. There isn't any object that says it's not fit to be part of the Mozart universe. But you don't create it with objects. The main function of objects is to create a transformation of the space. On the most primitive level, that's what happens: you open the space and you close the space. I truly believe that's why we go to the theater. Because when you go to the movies, the screen is always there, always in the same place. And of course with Shakespeare, there was nothing else—there was a little curtain, and it opened and it closed. And when you're at the Met there's a much bigger curtain, and all of a sudden you look into deep space. And it's exciting, it's the main device that you have, and that's what architects have as well. And that's how a medieval city is built: you walk through narrow streets and all of a sudden there is a square, and your heart just sinks. But in a way, you take the audience on that journey in that city, except that you're sitting in one place and the city moves around you.

When you hear Wagner's *Funeral March* it's very difficult—even though totally possible—to rap to it. Or let's compare the funeral march with an aria from *Figaro*: it's difficult to dance it the way you dance to *Figaro*. *The Funeral March* makes you move in a different way. It's all about the rhythm.

On the set designer as choreographer

Set designer or choreographer—it's the same. We're doing a similar job. Choreographers are working with human bodies, and in a way I'm also working with human bodies. The bodies have to move inside or merge. The way Vsevolod Meyerhold was thinking of theater, it completely merges—the set and the human bodies. And I constantly strive for that ideal. That's why I feel so close to choreography. I don't choreograph every single second; I have to choreograph in bigger strokes.

Biography

George Tsypin is a sculptor, architect, and designer of opera, film, and video. He won an International Competition of "New and Spontaneous Ideas for the Theater for Future Generations" some 20 years ago. Since then his opera designs have been seen all over the world, including the Salzburg Festival; Opéra de Bastille, Paris; Covent Garden, London; La Scala, Milan; and the Metropolitan Opera, New York. He has worked in all major theaters in America, and in the Nineties expanded his work to include design for film, television, concerts, exhibitions, and installations. The first personal gallery show of his sculpture took place in 1991 at Twining Gallery, New York. He created the Planet Earth Gallery, one of the Millennium Projects in the UK: a major installation of moving architectural elements, videos, and 200 sculptures. He also exhibited his work at Venice Biennale in 2002. Tsypin studied architecture in Moscow and theater design in New York and has won numerous awards. He has worked for many years with renowned directors such as Julie Taymor, Peter Sellars, Francesca Zambello, Jürgen Flimm, and Andrei Konchalovsky, and has a special creative relationship with the conductor Valery Gergiev. His book *George Tsypin Opera Factory: Building in the Black Void* was published in 2005.

Robert Wilson

Set and Lighting Design

World-renowned theater artist Robert Wilson is both a director and a designer. Best known for his original work *Einstein on the Beach*, he was Heiner Müller's favorite director because of their diverse backgrounds and differences, which created a healthy artistic "conflict" and collaboration. In speaking about the theater, Wilson looks at another conflict on the theater stage: between Western realism and realistic representations and Eastern formalized and codified ones. Additionally, he highlights the primary importance of light and lighting design for his stage directing and stage design.

Madama Butterfly, Giacomo Puccini.
Opera Bastille, Paris, France, 1993. Directed by Robert Wilson. Set design: Robert Wilson. Lighting design: Heinrich Brunke and Robert Wilson. The stage is created as a theater image with a precise composition of figures, and with specific codified postures, gestures, and lighting. The cyclorama is lit with blue light for the background (Act II).

Introduction

Robert Wilson has his own approach not only to design, but also to directing. He explains how he layers his productions, creating the visual images first and then superimposing the text and sound on top. He likens this multi-layered process to architecture, explaining how the different layers interact in order to complete the picture. Additionally, he discusses his one-man production of *Hamlet* to illustrate his directing technique. He also criticizes the Western theater for giving too much importance to realism, and discusses the more traditional forms of Eastern theater as an alternative.

For Wilson, lights hold a very important part in both the design and directing of each production, and he discusses the role of light, pointing out that he uses lights as early on as the first rehearsals.

Aida, Giuseppe Verdi.

Covent Garden, London, UK, 2003. Directed by Robert Wilson. Set and lighting design: Robert Wilson. Note the specific lighting on downstage figures bringing out and highlighting the costumes, figures, and faces (Act II, Scene 2).

"The structure is just a frame to get you somewhere else. It's how you fill in the structure that's important."

Approach

I usually start with a structure. My *Hamlet* has a symmetrical structure, and it begins with, "Had I but time ... but let it be." Those are the last words of *Hamlet*, and the rest is silence. So that's a frame. And then I divided it into so many parts—a visual outline. It starts with a pile of rocks, and the pile of rocks is reduced and there are two columns, the two women in his life. There's Ophelia, and Ophelia's scene was divided into four parts; and then there's Gertrude, and that scene is divided into four parts. So those are two structural columns that bridge this arc of Hamlet's words.

Occasionally I do some costumes myself, but I usually work closely with a costume designer. In this case, I worked with Frida Parmigiani, and she knew that I was playing all the parts, so I had to be Gertrude and I had to be Ophelia. I wore a basic suit, and sometimes I took the jacket off and changed it. At the end I had a trunk and I took all the clothes of all the characters out of the trunk. And then I threw them all over the stage, except for Ophelia's and Gertrude's. Finally I threw the mother's dress in the middle of the stage. But I held on to Ophelia's, I couldn't throw hers. And I say these words for Ophelia: "Truth be a liar, but never doubt, I loved." And that's why I couldn't throw her dress. Her dress was left on the proscenium. It all has a sort of mathematical structure.

But the structure itself is boring; the structure is just a frame to get you somewhere else. It's how you fill in the structure that's important. I do all of the visuals first. And I do all of the movements for the scene silently, and it's videotaped. In this case I had my co-director, Ann-Christin Rommen, notate all the movements that I had done as improvisations, and then I had to go back and learn it all, and that took three years.

The first time you do something it's spontaneous, but it takes many, many times to free yourself. Like Charlie Chaplin, for example. Chaplin would do 150 to 200 takes on a scene. He worked on a film for a year, and he did it over and over and over to get it right, to make it free. I, too, have to break things down, learn it technically. Where is my weight? How should I adjust here? Where does it change there?

I do it all silently, then I go back and put text over that, and I usually have someone read the text and watch and notate the movements. Or I look at the videotape and read the text, then I put the text to the movement. But above all the visual look is first. Most directors find a text, then they figure out what to do with it. I put the text aside. The text is like a radio drama, and the play is like a silent movie, and somehow you put the two together. Sometimes it works, sometimes it doesn't. I don't want to illustrate the text.

"I don't do stage decoration. I do architecture."

The Magic Flute, Wolfgang Amadeus Mozart.

Opera Bastille, Paris, France, 1991. Directed by Robert Wilson. Set and lighting design: Robert Wilson. Costume design: John Conklin. Blue-lit triangle and square against blue backdrop (Act I, Scene 15).

The Magic Flute, Wolfgang Amadeus Mozart.

Opera Bastille, Paris, France, 1991. Directed by Robert Wilson. Set and lighting design: Robert Wilson. Costume design: John Conklin. Note the use of lighting focused on the figures and faces to create the stage image (Act II).

I've worked with many authors. I've worked with Christopher Knowles, I've worked with Heiner Müller, Euripides, Susan Sontag, William Burroughs, Virginia Woolf, Anton Chekov, Henrik Ibsen—I just did Ibsen.

Structuring and layering the design

To develop the images, I draw it, structure it. When I did *Einstein on the Beach,* I did three things: a train, a trial, and a field. The train in the last scene is different from the train in the first scene. It is seen from a different perspective. But it is all structured.

It has an architectural structure: vertical lines to horizontal lines, dark spaces to light spaces. I don't see what I do visually as decoration or illustration; 95 percent of what you see in Western theater is illustration. People who do lights are decorating a play. People who do sets are decorating a play. I don't do stage decoration. I do architecture. So the light can have its own rhythm, the text can have its own structure and rhythm, the movements can have their own rhythm, the stage set can have its own rhythm and structure. And all of these things are layered together like transparent, stratified zones that are placed together. They can be independent of one another, but in the end they're structured together. So it's not arbitrary why one thing is placed next to another. It's as if what I'm seeing helps me to hear. Usually what you're seeing is just there to second what you're hearing, as in Western theater. With the classical theater in Japan and China and India and Africa, and the Eskimos and Latin Americans—it's just not that way. It's been passed on through tradition: a visual language for theater. If you do a 14th-century Noh play, the movements have been notated since the 14th century and you learn them. You start learning them when you're two years old; it's a theatrical language. If you're a Balinese dancer, there are hundreds of ways of moving your eyes; it's a theatrical language that you learn. If you're in the Peking Opera, there's a way of moving the sleeve of your costume; and it's something you start learning when you're two or three years old, and you're learning it all your life. It's a theatrical language.

I have my own theatrical language, and I've been learning it over time and use it to create these structures.

On choice of work

I do things that complement each other. I have done Flaubert's *The Temptation of St. Anthony* scored with the songs and lyrics of Dr. Bernice Johnson Reagan. She's an African-American scholar and composer who comes from a deeply spiritual background. *2Lips and dancers and space*, a ballet I just did with the Netherlands Dance Theater III, is going to open a festival in Holland. It has a text by Christopher Knowles that is sometimes nonsensical, a play with words—more like concrete poetry, really. Then I do Ibsen. So, these are very different authors and they complement each other.

For example, I will work with Lou Reed, who is very loud. And right after that I will work with Luigi Nono, and his work is very, very quiet; it's more meditative. So the loudness of Reed becomes clearer because I am now doing Nono.

In one season in Germany I did Virginia Woolf's *Orlando* at the Schaubühne, then at the Kammerspiele in Munich I did Chekhov, then I did Tom Waits and William Burroughs in Hamburg. Three completely different works.

On naturalism and artificiality

At the Kammerspiele I did Chekhov's *Swan Song* with a very naturalistic set. It looked like a set from the late 19th-century Russian theater: a wooden set with a backstage area. The gestures were somewhat more naturalistic. But nothing is "natural" to me on stage. I think naturalism is a lie and anything on stage is artificial.

I just went to see a play by Tennessee Williams. It was so stupid, because these actors think they're acting "naturally," but it's not natural to be on stage; it's artificial. If you accept that you're doing something artificially, you'll be much more natural while doing it. If you say, even if you want it to look naturalistic, "Okay, what I'm doing is artificial," then you have a different place in your mind. There's an honesty that exists, which doesn't exist if you believe you're being natural and you're on stage trying to act naturally.

When Marlon Brando was young, he was a very formalistic actor. In his first play in 1947 he walked on stage and stood for five minutes and didn't move, and the audience was paralyzed. This, you know, is the power of a man who knew how to stand on stage. He knew how to simply pick up a hat and touch it. It was a central thing, a formalistic thing. He was coming out of a school that wanted to do psychological, naturalistic theater. But in a way—especially in his earlier work—his approach was very formal, very crafted.

The Magic Flute, Wolfgang Amadeus Mozart.

Opera Bastille, Paris, France, 1991. Directed by Robert Wilson. Set and lighting design: Robert Wilson. Costume design: John Conklin. Codified postures and gestures combine with precise lighting (Act II).

The Magic Flute, Wolfgang Amadeus Mozart.

Opera Bastille, Paris, France, 1991. Directed by Robert Wilson. Set and lighting design: Robert Wilson. Costume design: John Conklin. The repetition of the triangle motif for the set (Act II).

Madama Butterfly, Giacomo Puccini. *Opera Bastille, Paris, France, 1993. Directed by Robert Wilson. Set design: Robert Wilson. Lighting design: Heinrich Brunke and Robert Wilson. A yellow-and-red-lit backdrop creates the atmosphere for this scene in* Madama Butterfly *(Act I).*

Madama Butterfly, Giacomo Puccini. *Opera Bastille, Paris, France, 1993. Directed by Robert Wilson. Set design: Robert Wilson. Lighting design: Heinrich Brunke and Robert Wilson.* Madama Butterfly *with blue-lit background (Act I).*

Aida, Giuseppe Verdi.

Covent Garden, London, UK, 2003. Directed by Robert Wilson. Set and lighting design: Robert Wilson. A desolate, desert-like landscape created with pale orange lighting. Note singers standing in stylized and codified postures. Also note the counterpoint created by the blue dress against the warm background (Act III).

Aida, Giuseppe Verdi.

Covent Garden, London, UK, 2003. Directed by Robert Wilson. Set and lighting design: Robert Wilson. Vertical, rectangular shapes and stylized figure create the stage image (Act IV, Scene 1).

"Light is the most essential element in the theater—the element that helps us hear and see better."

On creating images, pace, and light

I don't know where the images that I create come from. I can look out the window and see something. I can sit and something comes to me. I can look in a magazine; I can look in a book. The world is a library, it's all around you, and you just draw from whatever sources. The building in *Einstein on the Beach* is the one I see out of the window of my loft. But there's no one way.

As for pace, I find it by repeating it over and over. Rhythm is about timing, and timing is something you find by doing it many, many, many times.

And without light, there's no space. Light is the most essential element in the theater—the element that helps us hear and see better. Usually light is a distraction for me when I go to the theater. The lighting for *Einstein* isn't done two or three weeks before you open. It's part of the architecture; it's structured. I work with light, and it's the very first thing I do. In rehearsal with the actors or whatever, it is light that I do—it's always something with the light. It's sketched and drawn from the very beginning. And I work with it in all my rehearsals. I just started *A Winter's Tale* in Berlin for the Berliner Ensemble. The first thing I did was light the space. I don't know what's going to happen next. I have no ideas yet. I try to empty my head, because I don't want to know. Then I light the space, and then I ask an actor to go onto the set and do something; and then I have someone else do something, and sometimes I'll make a series of cues for light. I don't know what's going to happen in that space and I don't want to know right away. Once I know what a space looks like, it's easier for me to know what to do within it.

Delving beneath the surface

When I'm making a work for the theater, I try to make an overall structure first. For any work that I've done, I can usually tell you the structure in less than a minute. I try to see the whole, big thing. It's not important, if you understand the structure of Mozart, to appreciate the music; it's how you play the music that's important. But without the structure, the music probably couldn't have been written. Once I have a structure, then I can be much freer to fill it in. Theater has to be about one thing first, and then it can be about a million things. But if it's not about one thing, it's too complicated.

Hamlet has to be about one thing, and you have to see the whole quickly. And then you break it down. It's like a body: the mystery's in the surface, and the surface is the skin, and beneath the skin you have meat and bones. So I start with the surface—something very simple. As you go on, you get into more complexities. But if you come back to the surface after a long period of rehearsal, the surface will resonate in a different way. You still try to keep it simple, but it resonates in a different way because you've been through the rehearsal time, and through the meat and the bones in the works.

I've done a lot of opera over the last years: *The Magic Flute*, the *Ring Cycle* twice, *Madama Butterfly* in Paris, Moscow, and Los Angeles, and *Parsifal* in Los Angeles with Placido Domingo. But I don't prefer opera to theater. I just do both.

Biography

Robert Wilson arrived in New York in 1963 to attend Brooklyn's Pratt Institute. Soon afterward, with his Byrd Hoffman School of Byrds, he developed his first signature works, including *King of Spain*, *Deafman Glance*, *The Life and Times of Joseph Stalin*, and *A Letter for Queen Victoria*. He then turned his attention to large-scale opera and, with Philip Glass, created *Einstein on the Beach* in 1976, which achieved worldwide acclaim and altered conventional notions of a moribund form. In collaboration with internationally renowned writers and performers, Wilson then created landmark original works at the Festival d'Automne, Paris; Schaubühne, Berlin; Thalia Theater, Hamburg; and the Salzburg Festival. He has also applied his striking formal language to the operatic repertoire, including *Parsifal*, Hamburg and Houston; *The Magic Flute*, *Madama Butterfly*, and *Lohengrin*, the Metropolitan Opera, New York.

Wilson recently completed *I La Galigo*, an entirely new production based on an epic poem from Indonesia, which toured extensively and appeared at the Lincoln Center Festival in the summer of 2005. His drawings, furniture designs, and installations have also been shown in museums and galleries internationally. Wilson's awards and honors include two Guggenheim Fellowship Awards in 1971 and 1980, the Rockefeller Foundation Fellowship Award in 1975, a nomination for the Pulitzer Prize in Drama in 1986, the Golden Lion for sculpture from the Venice Biennale in 1993, the Dorothy and Lillian Gish Prize for lifetime achievement in 1996, the Premio Europa Award from Taormina Arte in 1997, election to the American Academy of Arts and Letters in 2000, the National Design Award for lifetime achievement in 2001, and Commandeur des arts et des lettres in 2002.

Credits

John Lee Beatty

A Delicate Balance (sketches)
Courtesy of John Lee Beatty
A Delicate Balance (photo)
Photo by Joan Marcus
The Rivals
Courtesy of John Lee Beatty
Burn This
Courtesy of John Lee Beatty
The Caretaker (sketches and model)
Courtesy of John Lee Beatty

Howell Binkley

Jersey Boys
Courtesy of Howell Binkley
Dracula
Courtesy of Howell Binkley

John Conklin

The Ring Cycle, San Francisco Opera
Photos by Ron Scherl
The Ring Cycle (models)
Courtesy of John Conklin
The Ring Cycle, Chicago Lyric Opera
Photos by Dan Rest

Beverly Emmons

Aladdin
Courtesy of Beverly Emmons
Twelfth Night
Courtesy of Beverly Emmons
A Midsummer Night's Dream
Courtesy of Beverly Emmons
Einstein on the Beach
Photo by Johann Elbers

Susan Hilferty

Too Clever By Half
(photos and drawings)
Courtesy of Susan Hilferty
The Seagull (photo)
Courtesy of Susan Hilferty
Wicked (drawings)
Courtesy of Susan Hilferty
Jitney (drawing)
Courtesy of Susan Hilferty

Constance Hoffman

A Midsummer Night's Dream
Photos by Richard Termine
A Midsummer Night's Dream
(drawings)
Courtesy of Constance Hoffman

Ming Cho Lee

Mourning Becomes Elektra
Photos by Carol Rosegg
La Boheme (sketch and models)
Courtesy of Ming Cho Lee
King John
Photo by Carol Rosegg
Peer Gynt (model)
Courtesy of Ming Cho Lee
Annie
Courtesy of Naples Museum of Art
King Lear (sketch and model)
Courtesy of Ming Cho Lee

Adrianne Lobel

On the Town
Courtesy of Adrianne Lobel
Dr. Atomic
Courtesy of San Francisco Opera

Santo Loquasto

Faust (models)
Courtesy of the Metropolitan Opera Technical Department
Faust
Photos by Marty Sohl

Jennifer Tipton

Hamlet
Photos by Lea Xiao
As You Like It
Photo by T. Charles Erickson
Electric Haiku
Photos by Lea Xiao
Hansel and Gretal
Photo by Larry Merkle for San Francisco Opera

George Tsypin

Waiting for the Barbarians
Courtesy of George Tsypin
Adriana Mater
Courtesy of George Tsypin
Grendel
Courtesy of George Tsypin
The Ring Cycle
Courtesy of George Tsypin
West Side Story
Courtesy of George Tsypin
The Magic Flute
Courtesy of George Tsypin

Robert Wilson

Madama Butterfly
Courtesy of the Byrd Hoffman Foundation
Aida
Courtesy of the Byrd Hoffman Foundation
The Magic Flute
Courtesy of the Byrd Hoffman Foundation

Index